THE WISDOM OF ORDER

An Exploration of Lonergan's *Method in Theology*

The Wisdom of Order

An Exploration of Lonergan's
Method in Theology

JOHN D. DADOSKY

UNIVERSITY OF TORONTO PRESS
Toronto Buffalo London

© University of Toronto Press 2024
Toronto Buffalo London
utorontopress.com

ISBN 978-1-4875-5445-3 (cloth)   ISBN 978-1-4875-5446-0 (EPUB)
                                  ISBN 978-1-4875-5447-7 (PDF)

Lonergan Studies

___

Library and Archives Canada Cataloguing in Publication

Title: The wisdom of order : an exploration of Lonergan's Method in theology / John D. Dadosky.
Names: Dadosky, John D., 1966–, author.
Series: Lonergan studies.
Description: Series statement: Lonergan studies | Includes bibliographical references and index.
Identifiers: Canadiana (print) 20240329171 | Canadiana (ebook) 20240329198 | ISBN 9781487554453 (cloth) | ISBN 9781487554460 (EPUB) | ISBN 9781487554477 (PDF)
Subjects: LCSH: Lonergan, Bernard J.F. Method in theology. | LCSH: Theology – Methodology.
Classification: LCC BR118 .D33 2024 | DDC 230/.201 – dc23

___

Cover design: John Beadle
Cover image: Labyrinth of Chartres Cathedral (Cathédrale Notre-Dame de Chartres). Sylvain Sonnet/The Image Bank Unreleased via Getty Images.

We wish to acknowledge the land on which the University of Toronto Press operates. This land is the traditional territory of the Wendat, the Anishnaabeg, the Haudenosaunee, the Métis, and the Mississaugas of the Credit First Nation.

University of Toronto Press acknowledges the financial support of the Government of Canada, the Canada Council for the Arts, and the Ontario Arts Council, an agency of the Government of Ontario, for its publishing activities.

This book has been published with the help of a grant from the Federation for the Humanities and Social Sciences, through the Awards to Scholarly Publications Program, using funds provided by the Social Sciences and Humanities Research Council.

To four teachers, mentors, colleagues, and friends from Regis College who supported and encouraged me in my career: Carl Starkloff, SJ (d. 2007), Margaret Brennan, IHM (d. 2016), Ovey Mohammed, SJ (d. 2020), and Robert M. Doran, SJ (d. 2021)

Contents

Preface xi

Introduction 3
   Ordered Unity 3
   Method and the Pluralistic Context 4
   The Scope of This Work 6

1 Approaching Lonergan's *Method in Theology*: The Preface and Introduction 7
   The Preface 7
   The Introduction 9
   Theology and Mediation 9
      Theology Mediates through Mutual Self-Mediation 14
   An Empirical Notion of Culture 17
   Method Defined 21
   A Model? 22

2 Method 23
   A Third Way 23
   Method 24
   Excursus on Transcendental Beauty 32
   Transcendental Method 35
   Functions of Transcendental Method 36

3 Apprehending and Doing the Good 44
   The Good 45
   Skills 45
   Feelings 47
   Excursus: Beauty and Intersubjectivity 48
   The Scale of Values 49
      Distorted Affectivity 54

The Notion of Value 55
Judgments of Value 56
*Some Clarifications Regarding Lonergan's
    Fourth-Level Operations* 59
Crowe's Development of Contemplation 62
Fourth-Level Operations: Insights? 63
Beliefs 64
The Structure of the Human Good 70
Progress and Decline 71

4 Different Types of Meaning 74
Types of Meaning 74
  Intersubjectivity and Intersubjective Meaning 74
  Intersubjective Meaning 75
  Linguistic Meaning 78
  Incarnate Meaning 79
Elements of Meaning 79
  Functions of Meaning 81
Four Realms and "Four" Stages of Meaning 83
  First Stage to Second Stage 84
  Second Stage to Third Stage 86
Transcendence and the Fourth Stage 90
  The Fourth Stage: Some Questions 96

5 Lonergan's Notion of "Genuine" Religion 100
The Question of God 101
Self-Transcendence 102
  A Note on Kierkegaard and the Negative
    Aesthetic 103
Religious Experience 104
Expressions of Religious Experience 105
*Religious Development Is Dialectical: Distortions of
    Religion* 109
The Word 111
Faith 112
Religious Belief 113
Technical Note 114
*Genuine Religion and the Fourth Stage as a
    Differentiated Realm* 117

6 Ordered Wisdom: The Eight Functional Specialties 121
Three Types of Specialization 121
An Eightfold Division 122

Grounds of the Division 126
The Need for the Division 128
Dynamic Unity 129
Conclusion 132

Notes 133

Bibliography 147

Index 155

Preface

In October 1990, on the grounds of the picturesque St. Meinrad Seminary in south-central Indiana, I fell in love with the thought of Bernard Lonergan (1904–84). It was a beautiful autumn day, and I was sitting on a picnic table, overlooking scenic pastures and reading an article assigned by my professor, Sr. Carmel McEnroy, RSM (d. 2019), for a foundations course. The article was Lonergan's "Theology in Its New Context," and it changed my life.[1] At the time, the seminary was experiencing deep divisions between various factions. As I read Lonergan's insights in that article, it occurred to me that there was no turning back from what Vatican II had inaugurated. I also realized that one could not afford to simply cast aside tradition. Lonergan's emphasis upon new theological foundations as a reflection on personal conversion was for me a refreshing and paradigmatic insight.

Several years later, I would encounter another significant article, Karl Rahner's "Towards a Fundamental Interpretation of Vatican II," while in Professor Dennis Doyle's ecclesiology class at the University of Dayton. Together, these two articles have profoundly influenced my theological thinking. Indeed, it was a highlight of my career when I could revisit Rahner's article in my own appropriation, invoking Lonergan's work in my own appropriation "Towards a Fundamental Re-interpretation of Vatican II" – with all due credit given to Rahner, of course. Moreover, to have the honour of editing "Theology in Its New Context" for volume 13 of the *Collected Works of Bernard Lonergan* served for me as confirmation, as St. Ignatius Loyola might say, of my vocation to Lonergan studies.

I had entered the seminary to discern a vocation; paradoxically, I left at the end of the academic year with a different vocation in hand – the life-long study of Bernard Lonergan. I enrolled in the master's program in theological studies at the University of Dayton the following fall. I was encouraged in my interest by Prof. Rev. Jack McGrath, SM (d. 2015). For his seminar course on contemporary theologians, I prepared a lecture on Lonergan's *Method in Theology*. This was before PowerPoint presentations, so I created my own charts: four levels of consciousness; four transcendental precepts corresponding to eight functional specialties. My passion for communicating Lonergan's genius came through to my peers and my professor. At the end of the lecture, Prof. McGrath stated, "I believe Bernard Lonergan is sitting on a cloud smiling right now." As recently as 2017, I was giving a similar lecture to graduate students at Regis College. I was taken aback when one Jesuit student made virtually the same comment.

In the library of the University of Dayton, I gazed with perplexity on Robert Doran's then recent tome *Theology and the Dialectics of History* (1990). Eventually, I moved to Regis College in Toronto to do doctoral studies under Doran and another Jesuit, Carl Starkloff. I had been very interested in Doran's creative work with Lonergan and depth psychology. In Toronto I worked as an assistant in the Lonergan Research Institute, cataloguing about 80 per cent of Lonergan's personal archives, an initiative started by Doran and Frederick Crowe. I completed my doctorate in 2001 and joined the Regis College faculty in the same year. I am very grateful to the Canadian Jesuits for the opportunity to teach and research on Lonergan at the Jesuit school for over twenty years. One highlight of my career was to co-edit the *Collected Works* edition of *Method in Theology* (vol. 14) with Robert Doran.

Lonergan once declared to a room of his followers, "I hope you all become good non-disciples." Relatedly, Prof. Cyril Orji, who has written prolifically on Lonergan, describes encountering two antagonists in his career: the Lonergan despisers and the Lonergan extremists.[2] To this could be added the Lonergan opportunists, those who affiliate with his thought but without a real commitment to it or ability/willingness to understand it correctly. Unfortunately, all too often the tremendous value that people encounter in Lonergan's thought can also be distorted by the very ideas Lonergan campaigned against throughout his life, such as inauthenticity. Along these lines, the Lonergan "purists" would do well to take Lonergan's admonition to his followers to heart. The Lonergan despisers, I find, have often read little or none of his work. The opportunists apprehend something of value in his thought but are unable, for various reasons, to appropriate it.

In my experience, a genuine call to Lonergan studies can be a solitary venture for the scholars who devote significant time and effort to his thought.[3] Nevertheless, Lonergan conceived method in theology to be a collaborative enterprise. But researchers do not write for the current generation only: rather, they hope that the seeds of their work will bear fruit in future generations.

I want to thank Regis College (now the Regis-St. Michael's Faculty of Theology as of 2022) for a research leave during the fall of 2021 to write this book. I am grateful to Len Husband and the editors of University of Toronto Press for their support of this project and to the Federation for the Humanities and Social Sciences for a publication subsidy through the Awards to Scholarly Publications Program, using funds provided by the Social Sciences and Humanities Research Council of Canada. Riley McGuire read over an earlier version and gave invaluable suggestions.

The year 2022 marked the fiftieth anniversary of the first publication of Bernard Lonergan's *Method in Theology*. This exploration of that book, which I first discovered thirty-two years ago, is the fruit of my own years of teaching, research, exploration, and development of Lonergan's thought. This book is the first of two volumes. This volume addresses the first part of *Method in Theology*, and the second volume will address the second part of the book. I often tell my students: "On the one hand, Lonergan is not for everyone; on the other hand, Lonergan *is* for everyone." My hope is that, as the genius of Lonergan's methodological breakthrough takes deeper roots in Christian theology, one day – perhaps when a pope christens his achievements – his work will be applied and developed throughout the church as the application of a wisdom of order.

John Dadosky
26 November 2022
Regis-St. Michael's Faculty of Theology, Toronto

THE WISDOM OF ORDER

Introduction

"Vital, intelligent, reasonable, responsible, *mine* and Catholic[!]" These words were handwritten at the bottom of the notes of 5 February 1965 where Bernard Lonergan (1904–84) recorded the most important insight(s) of his career and perhaps for the future of Catholic theology – the breakthrough to eightfold functional specialization that he would later take up in *Method in Theology*.[1] The eight functional specialties (research, interpretation, history, dialectic, foundations, doctrines, systematics, and communications) were developed to ameliorate the problem of specialization silos and to promote an interdisciplinary, dynamic, and collaborative unity within theological research. Lonergan's famous insight was not spontaneous: rather, it was the fruit of years of thinking about the question, stretching back to his dissertation. Frederick Crowe describes his pursuit as a "Herculean effort of thirty-four years that produced *Method in Theology*."[2] It is perhaps no coincidence that the closing of the Second Vatican Ecumenical Council in 1965 coincided with the year of Lonergan's methodological insight. Vatican II was a breakthrough council, although the extent to which it was a watershed has been widely debated. Karl Rahner's hermeneutics of the council as the church's coming of age as a world church will likely endure as a primary interpretation.[3] I want to situate the importance of Lonergan's achievement, as documented in his *Method in Theology*, as it addresses two points raised at Vatican II.

Ordered Unity

Lonergan's achievement addresses the challenge of the fragmentation of knowledge, characteristic of our age, which arises as knowledge becomes increasingly specialized in a context of increasing religious-cultural pluralism. Such fragmentation can only be met by a wisdom of order.⁴ Specifically and perhaps unwittingly, Lonergan, "thinking with the church" as St. Ignatius might put it, addressed the question put forth in *Gaudium et spes*: "How can we quickly and progressively harmonize the proliferation of particular branches of study with the necessity of forming a synthesis of them, and of preserving among [human beings] the faculties of contemplation and observation which lead to wisdom?"⁵ *Method in Theology* aims at forming that dynamic synthesis between various branches in theology without succumbing to the philosophical complacency of our age, where such complacency involves a devaluing of philosophical reasoning, an elevation of doubt, and a rejection of metaphysics.⁶

Lonergan's conception of a structure of eight methodological specialties provides a provocative and sober anecdote to the fragmentation of knowledge with its increasing expanse of data, where researchers say "more and more about less and less."⁷

Method and the Pluralistic Context

Method in Theology would also meet the principal requirements for the course Vatican II called for in foundational theology. In the same year as Lonergan's 1965 breakthrough insight, *Optatam totius*, the "Decree on Priestly Formation," was promulgated at the Second Vatican Council. This document would attempt to reshape theological education by insisting on the "integration of philosophy and theology." As part of this integration, it proposed an introductory course that would attempt to address the philosophical and theological disciplines, introducing students to the mystery of salvation and their personal appropriation of that mystery.⁸ However, according to Rahner, seeking such an integration between philosophy and theology in an introductory course is complicated because of pluralism in both theological disciplines and philosophical views.⁹ Here we find Lonergan's contribution in *Method in Theology* meets both difficulties mentioned by Rahner, in addition to one he does not mention – religious pluralism.

Lonergan addresses diverse philosophical views in chapters 1 and 3 of *Method in Theology*. However, those chapters rest on a foundation laid earlier in his philosophical tome *Insight: A Study of Human Understanding* (1957). Indeed, Lonergan's entire life project includes a subtle, consistent, and profound response to pluralism in its many forms. To be sure, this does not mean he accepts all forms of pluralism willy-nilly. As we will see, he challenges inauthentic attitudes that flow from a fourfold bias.

To elaborate further on philosophical pluralism, from the very outset of *Insight* Lonergan aims to provide a philosophical basis for pluralism that avoids relativism and scepticism. One is not forced to choose between the seemingly disparate worlds of everyday common sense and theory (mathematics and science), but rather, one discovers their commonality and difference by relating them to one another within one's interior consciousness. There is a common ground in human consciousness in which philosophical approaches can be grounded and understood. The common ground is the *generalized empirical method* of experience, understanding, judgment, and decision. Diverse fields of knowledge have their basis in various levels, patterns, and differentiations of consciousness. However, Lonergan is not naive. The radical (contradictory) differences between philosophical positions ultimately lies in the authenticity of the person through the greater or lesser existence of a fourfold bias; through grace, the blocks in development are subject to transformations and healings in consciousness. The extent to which one properly thematizes the generalized empirical method in one's own consciousness is the extent to which one can properly do theology. Conversely, mistakes in one's theology can be traced to a mistaken philosophy of mind. Lonergan demonstrates this in Christian history, referencing the example of the Stoicism of Tertullian and the Neoplatonism of Origen versus the implicit critical realism of Athanasius, the latter having championed the proper hermeneutics of *homoousios* following the Council of Nicaea (*CWL* 13, 200–20).

Method in Theology addresses the plurality of the theological disciplines by the dynamic unity of the functional specialties and the two phases of theology. The eightfold division has a mediating phase (with four specialties: research, interpretation, history, and dialectic) and a mediated phase (also with four specialties: foundations, doctrines, systematics, and communications). Moreover, two of these specialties (one in each phase) correlate and correspond to each one of the four levels of Lonergan's theory of intentional consciousness (experience, understanding, judgment, and decision), thus enabling him to separate each functional specialty in terms of the goal of a particular operation. For example, *interpretation* and *systematics* each correlate and correspond to the second level of intentional consciousness, *understanding*. The goal of *interpretation* is to understand a text; the goal of *systematics*, to understand the mysteries of the faith in a synthetic way, insofar as such mysteries can be understood.

As stated, in addition to the two types of pluralism Rahner mentioned, the German theologian could have included the pluralism of religious views in a multifaith context. This would indeed be a requirement for many who are beginning their theological formation today, who must carry out their professional careers in a religiously pluralistic context. As we will see, a key chapter in *Method in Theology* pertains to religion and provides Christians with a basis for creatively engaging religious pluralism.

The Scope of This Work

This book is at once a commentary on and an exploration of Lonergan's *Method in Theology*. It is a commentary, but one aimed at an exploration of further themes. Admittedly, many of the latter themes are based on my own questions, research, and scholarship over the years, which the reader will notice throughout the book. My aim is both to present my own work here as an exposition of Lonergan's masterful insights and to identify and explore themes Lonergan did not develop, or at least, I point to further areas of development.

When Robert Doran (1939–2021) and I were editing *Method in Theology* as volume 14 of the *Collected Works of Bernard Lonergan*, a number of questions arose for me that were not appropriate to explore in that critical edition. For example, Lonergan was undeveloped in his thoughts about transcendental beauty; the fourth level of operations, decision; and the role of dramatic bias (psychological wounds) in dialectical analysis, to name a few. I decided to explore the entire text, expositing to be sure, but with a view to indicating areas for further clarification and development. This book will focus on what Lonergan describes as the "background" chapters of the book (chaps. 1–5). Accordingly, I have divided this book into six chapters, with one chapter devoted to the preface and introduction, and the five remaining chapters corresponding to the first five chapters of Lonergan's *Method in Theology*. A second volume would address the "foreground chapters" of the latter text, engaging the chapters on the respective functional specialties (research, interpretation, history, dialectic, foundations, doctrines, systematics, and communications).

1 Approaching Lonergan's *Method in Theology*: The Preface and Introduction

"Method offers not rules to be followed blindly but a framework for creativity."
(*Method in Theology*, 4)

The preface and introduction to *Method in Theology* contain some important presuppositions for what Lonergan seeks to achieve in this text. These are concepts that Lonergan deemed necessary for introducing his work on functional specialization. I will focus on *mediation* as a two-way process and *the empirical notion of culture*. It is interesting how these two significant ideas make their way into the brief introduction, which Lonergan wrote last when composing the text. Before considering that, however, it is worthwhile saying something about the preface.

The Preface

Lonergan opens the preface to *Method in Theology*, published in 1972, with the statement "This book has long been in the making" (xv). Indeed, a historical study of the emergence of Lonergan's *Method* would span his entire career up to that point. He does not get explicitly serious about theological method until he completes his doctoral dissertation and begins his own forays into Thomas Aquinas's philosophy of knowledge and will.[1] Still, almost everything he wrote about up to that point appears in the fabric of *Method in Theology* to a greater or lesser

---

An earlier version of this chapter was presented at the Lonergan Graduate Seminar at Regis College, University of Toronto, on 17 October 2019. That version was published as "Mediation, Culture and Religion: Approaching Lonergan's *Method in Theology*," *The Lonergan Review* (Seton Hall University) 11, no. 1 (2020): 53–75, https://doi.org/10.5840/lonerganreview2020114.

degree. For example, his notion of religion in chapter 4 of *Method* is undergirded by his dissertation on Thomas Aquinas's notion of operative grace.[2]

David Tracy was the first to write a historical-theological study of Lonergan's intellectual development, in 1970. Tracy was one of Lonergan's prize students at the Gregorian University, and probably the most prolific and successful of his students at the Jesuit College in Rome. Although Tracy did not continue to pursue Lonergan's thought explicitly in his later work, Lonergan's influence stayed with him. Tracy had an intuition that something valuable was moving forward in Lonergan's work, and he documents it in his published doctoral dissertation *The Achievement of Bernard Lonergan*. The work traces the origins of Lonergan's philosophy of intentional consciousness from his doctoral dissertation through his formative insights leading to the threshold of *Method in Theology*. Tracy's work does not investigate Lonergan's contribution to specific topics in systematic theology – namely, his works on Trinity and Christology – nor does he engage his early works on history and economics. This is likely because none of these was central to the work of *Method in Theology* proper. In fact, the method Lonergan argues for rests on his own philosophy of conscious interiority developed in his earlier work *Insight: A Study of Human Understanding*.[3]

The second point Lonergan makes in the preface is to thank Regis College for giving him the time to write the book. In 1965, Lonergan had retired due to health reasons. He underwent a major operation, which entailed the removal of one of his lungs. He retired to Regis College, then located in the Willowdale neighbourhood of North York, Ontario, at that time a suburb of Toronto. Lonergan had the freedom to write, and, although deeply affected by these health issues, he felt a sense of urgency to complete the book. The reader of *Method in Theology* might do well to keep this in mind if she or he feels the book is cursory at points. It has been said that, whereas Lonergan's tome *Insight* is overwritten, *Method in Theology* is underwritten. Nonetheless, the most important insights Lonergan wanted to express most definitely make it into *Method in Theology*. The two chapters on history, for example, although not central to the book, enabled him to formulate ideas and interests that had been with him for some time (see *CWL* 25).

It is noteworthy that Lonergan completed his two principal works at Regis College. Early in his career he wrote *Insight* at the same college, albeit at a different location, in the early 1950s. This is significant for several reasons. First, Regis College is the Jesuit school of theology in Canada, which means his two most significant works belong to the Canadian intellectual heritage. Second, the University of Toronto Press's commitment to publish twenty-five volumes (recently completed) of his collected works attests to this historic legacy. It also means that Lonergan's Jesuit formation and his writing in a Jesuit context secure him a unique place in the history of the Jesuits in Canada. In the broader North American context, these secure him a special place in the Catholic intellectual life of the continent.

The Introduction

Having nearly completed the manuscript for *Method in Theology*, Lonergan struggled with what to say in the introduction. After mulling it over for a while, eventually he was challenged by a fellow Jesuit to simply write it. He went to his room and did so.[4] Although the introduction is brief, Lonergan offers a functional definition of theology, a commentary on the classicist notion of culture, a definition of method, the outline of the book, and some brief qualifications. Interestingly, the functional definition of theology, the first line – perhaps one of the most important – of the book, does not appear in any of his other writings or lectures on method up to that point.

Theology and Mediation

Lonergan gives a definition of theology in the opening line of the book: "A theology mediates between a cultural matrix and the significance and role of a religion in that matrix" (3). One might be thrown off a little by Lonergan's invocation of the terms "matrix" and "mediation," but the use of these technical terms likely signals his mathematical and philosophical background. A cultural matrix is simply the complex web of meanings and values that cohere among a community of people, generally, but not exclusively, bounded by a geographical space and/or a common language.

It is significant that Lonergan defines theology by *how* it functions rather than by the nature of its content. Anselm's *fides quaerens intellectum* (faith seeking understanding) is a famous example of the latter type of definition. It is not enough simply to have faith (in chapter 4, on religion, faith is approximately a knowledge of the supernatural): we want to understand what it is we believe insofar as the content of our faith can be understood (in the context of Lonergan's functional specialties, this is the task of *systematics*). By focusing on a functional definition, Lonergan brings the methodological aspect of the functional specialty systematics into play. Theology functions by mediating, as a stockbroker mediates between the investor and the stock market, or as a traffic officer mediates directions to multiple vehicles at an intersection. Theology is a mediation between the religion it reflects upon and the culture in which that reflection occurs. Still, culture and religion interpenetrate and blend in varying stages and contexts. Among other things, in the functional specialty *communications*, this means that theology is concretely an inculturation – the incarnation of the gospel into a specific context. And with regard to the functional specialty *systematics*, theology is to be guided by operations in interior consciousness (317).

A deeper question Lonergan does not address arises concerning the interaction between the mediation as inculturation in *communications*, on the one hand, and the mediation through operations in interior consciousness of *systematics*, on the other. In other words, to what extent will *systematics* provide a universally agreed-upon language in the world of Christians, like the universally agreed-upon language of mathematics and science, and to what extent will the vast contextual and global theologies contribute their unique cultural categories to enrich systematic theology? Does intercultural theology have more of a role to play in theology than simply the expression of the gospel in specific contexts (a major role of the functional specialty *communications* for Lonergan)? Does it also enrich systematic theology – the understanding of the mysteries of the faith? If so, in what ways? For example, if the Korean notion of *han*, an expression of deep existential suffering put forth by Minjung theologians, is able to mediate some deeper understanding of Christ's agony in the Garden, then could it have a more universal role to play in systematic theology as a whole when it comes to trying to understand the passion and death of Jesus? The question is open to further development.

Back to the matter of mediation. Let us try to get a more precise understanding of how this mediation occurs. Lonergan does not mean that this mediation is strictly one-way, as if the function of theology were simply to instruct or merely appropriate the cultural matrix. While Lonergan's intention is implicit in his writing, Robert Doran has explicated, and I agree with him, that the mediation between religion and culture in Lonergan is one of mutual self-mediation.[5] In this section, I will try to clarify this dynamic process.

The term "mediation" is defined by Lonergan in an earlier writing as "what comes in between; what somehow helps something else that is distinct."[6] If we were to apply this to the functional definition of theology as stated before, this would suggest that theology is a "go-between" arising from religion, but simultaneously a part of the cultural matrix from within. Presumably, this implies that mediation is a two-way process, and this has occurred throughout Christian history.

Lonergan uses "mediation" in several different senses throughout his writings. Moreover, his thinking developed over time. One of his first uses pertains to the different "realms of meaning": common sense, theory, interiority, and religion. These diverse modes of consciousness for the most part correlate with the operations in intentional consciousness and call for an integration from the standpoint of a single subject with a fourfold differentiated consciousness. Lonergan suggests that mediation plays a role in the integration, although he specifically emphasizes how the world of interiority can mediate to the world of common sense in order to make one's communication richer within that of the everyday world. Similarly, (religious) knowledge of God can be mediated (1) by the community, as in rituals, for example, (2) by the world of theory in reasonable and analogous speculations about the nature of God, and (3) by the world of interiority in the interior life of the mystic (*CWL* 6, 115–16). While Lonergan does not say it here, it follows that the sphere of religion, when fully developed, can mediate love and grace to the praxis of everyday living in the community (101).

In addition, Doran distinguishes Lonergan's use of mediation as *external* and *internal* to theology.[7] While one should not separate these two, it is a helpful distinction for our purposes here. The internal pertains to the differences between the two phases wherein the first is the mediating phase (research, interpretation, history, dialectic) engaging the past, and the second is the mediated phase (foundations, doctrines, systematics, communications) oriented to the future. The two phases operate through "reciprocal dependence" and with "dynamic interdependence and unity" (136–8).

For further clarification of what Lonergan has in mind for mediation external to theology, we advert to his more precise explanation later and Doran's development of that notion as applied to the functional definition of theology above. Briefly stated, Lonergan takes Aristotle as the basis of his understanding of mediation and generalizes it. Mediation for Aristotle pertains to the middle term of a syllogism that is the cause of the predicate in the subject. The middle term mediates between the first principle and the conclusions. Lonergan's idea for generalizing the notion of mediation from Aristotle's more specific use comes from Hegel's generalization of mediation, but Lonergan is quick to point out that he does not accept Hegel's idealist epistemology (*CWL* 6, 160–2).[8] Whereas Hegel extended mediation more broadly, Lonergan circumscribes it by appropriating from Aristotle the terms "immediate" and "mediate," where "immediate" refers to "a source, an origin, a ground, a basis" and "mediate" refers to "whatever results from it." The mediation may be "a result, consequence, outcome, insofar as it arises in a field of radiation, expansion, influence, insofar as it manifests, expresses, reveals, the basis." In terms of what he calls *simple mediation*, an example is the oxygen in the body immediate in the lungs and mediated to the rest of the body. Anger is immediate in the body but mediated through affectivity, expressions, and aggression. Truth is immediate in the first principles of a syllogism and mediated in the conclusions (CWL 6, 163, 174).

After explicating his notion of mediation, Lonergan goes on in "Mediation of Christ in Prayer" to distinguish several types of mediation: mutual mediation, self-mediation (which admits of three types), and mutual self-mediation.

Mutual mediation pertains to the various mediating parts of a "functioning whole." Lonergan provides the mechanical example of a watch, in which the balance wheel and the mainspring mutually mediate for the watch's proper functioning. Mutual mediation is more complex in the human body, where many more systems interact. Anger is immediate in one's affectivity but increases as one stews over a situation. Scientific method is a functioning whole between two immediate principles, empirical observation and intellectual inquiry; the two work together during experimentation, corroboration of hypotheses in the advance of scientific knowledge, and technological development (CWL 6, 166).

Whereas mutual mediation pertains to the functioning of "wholes," *self-mediation* pertains to the *development* of "wholes." The growth of a cell through division is a self-mediation. However, this development is not willy-nilly, but inheres in the potency of the organism itself based on underlying conditions. It develops in identifiable stages as unfolding through some internal law. This internal law or directed dynamism Lonergan calls *finality* because it is a movement towards some end or goal. "There is the structuring that regards both functioning at the moment and future functioning" (CWL 6, 167).

Finality directs the organism's development through a "process of specialization, of differentiation." It results in a greater complexity, to be sure, but the self-mediation of the organism also involves a "displacement upwards" that "involves the creation and exploitation of entirely new possibilities" (CWL 6, 168). The cells will be replaced, but the more complex organism of which they are a part continues on. For those familiar with Lonergan's theory of *emergent probability*, likely one of his most significant ideas, he has this in mind here (see CWL 3, chap. 4). Self-mediation involves development and there can be leaps in those developments as displacement upwards occurs in individuals and in species. A species self-mediates through reproduction. But species can come and go based on the underlying conditions for their existence.

When those conditions are met, the probability of the emergence of a species leap from a potentiality to an actuality. This is not the place to explore Lonergan's general and complex theory of emergent probability, but it is well to emphasize two things about self-mediation: it accounts for the development of "wholes," and it can be a collection of individual "wholes" – in other words, it can be communal.

Whereas an organism's biological development occurs through a displacement upwards, with the emergence of consciousness there is a "displacement inwards." Consciousness emerges with animal life, but this consciousness is driven by instinct and is extroverted. In human beings, however, there is a further development: "a deliberate transposition of center that occurs when one becomes a fully autonomous being" (*CWL* 6, 174). Human beings can deliberate and constitute themselves in the world through existential decisions. In human development, this occurs in two stages: (1) in childhood, as one's learning focuses mainly on objects, and (2) in adulthood, where one shifts from merely objects in the world to a recognition of free will and choice to constitute oneself in the world. "Such existential commitment is a disposal of oneself" (*CWL* 6, 171). Simultaneously, this disposition is to one's family, society, and transcendent value. Again, not only individuals self-mediate; communities do as well. The self-mediation of the individual occurs in one's living and the context of a community. The self-mediation of a community, as comprised of individuals who share common meanings and values, occurs in a shared lived history. The communities can explicitly constitute themselves in public statements, declarations, constitutions, creeds, and so on. There can also be development in those communities in their self-understanding.

This mutual interplay between individuals and communities raises the possibility of mutual self-mediation. The latter "is a function of interpersonal relations."[9] It pertains to the "immediate interpersonal situation" in which human beings find themselves. Mutual self-mediation complexifies the notion of mediation by bringing in the possibility of human beings interacting with one another. Examples of mutual self-mediation specifically mentioned by Lonergan include love and marriage, education in the home and in society, familial roles, friendships, and more formal relations such as mentors and authorities. He references Hegel's master-and-slave dialectic to suggest that the roles between human beings are not only reversable, but fluid and at times even destructive (*CWL* 6, 175).

Lonergan signals that mutual self-mediation is a source for creativity, drama, and literature (*CWL* 6, 176). This will make sense if we recall the various patterns of experience that Lonergan mentions in *Insight*.

In the practical world of common sense, for example, consciousness flows in a practical pattern of getting things done and/or consciousness flows in a dramatic pattern when dealing with other people. Such a world involves one's affectivity, mutual and conflicting desires, love, and hatred. I would even argue that the self-mediation of the individual contemplating an existential act of decision operates in a dramatic pattern insofar as he or she is exercising a basic freedom in an ephemeral context. While the decisions have a lasting significance, the temporality of existence heightens the sense of urgency to evaluate and deliberate, especially as one grows older. It is perhaps in such a context that we can understand another line from the same section of *Insight*: Lonergan's statement that "dramatic artistry" is a person's first act of living (*CWL* 3, 21). The making of oneself and interacting with others draws on a creative element of the psyche that charges our lives with meaning, affectivity, and value.

Theology Mediates through Mutual Self-Mediation

For Lonergan, theology "exhibits mutual mediation" (*CWL* 24, 142). His specification is that this occurs when it functions *internally*; namely: (1) as the mediation of his basic philosophy within the method of theology, a topic he deals with in chapter 1 of *Method in Theology*, insofar as his basic philosophy provides the basis for the eight functional specialties; and (2) as the various functional specialties mediate between each other, as in the principle of reciprocal dependence mentioned earlier.

Although not always explicitly stated, it is clear that Lonergan conceived of theology as mediation to be a two-way street, especially with respect to mediation external to theology. In an important essay originally conceived of as a chapter of *Method in Theology*, Lonergan states: "Not only does the cultural context influence theology to undo its past achievements, and make new demands upon it. But also, theology is called upon to influence the cultural context, to translate the word of God and so project it into new mentalities and new situations."[10] Doran has argued that the thrust of Lonergan's *Method in Theology* does not fully specify the mutual interplay between religion and culture.[11] First, there is no explicit example in *Method* of Lonergan's treatment of mutual self-mediation as communal. However, in "The Mediation of Christ in Prayer," he does refer to the education of children as one example of mutual self-mediation (*CWL* 6, 175). This would be communal as it implies a community of teachers active throughout the life of the child in bringing about the child's formation and education in a mutually self-mediating interaction with teachers, other students, and family members. Moreover, while it is clear for Lonergan that communities self-mediate, we can presume they can mutually self-mediate with other communities. Likewise, Doran has argued that mutual self-mediation is the proper way of construing how theology mediates *ad extra* between the cultural matrix and the significance and role of religion in that matrix. This implies, among other things, that the church is a learning church and not just a teaching one.[12] Although Doran points out that Lonergan's treatment in the functional specialty *communications* emphasizes a one-way street from the church to the context,[13] this minimal explication can be understood as the result of Lonergan's haste in completing the book, rather than his opposition to mutual self-mediation. Lonergan's Jesuit training would have disposed him to "find God in all things," a basic principle of Ignatian spirituality. Doran argues that the recognition of the universal mission of the Holy Spirit is the condition for discovering the fruits of the Spirit in cultures and in religions, a key opening for Ignatian discernment.[14]

The explicit recognition in theology of a mutual self-mediating relationship between religion and culture is paradigmatic. Moreover, while the idea has existed since the beginning of the church, the first official recognition that the church has mutual self-mediating relations with other religions, cultures, and Christian denominations occurs at Vatican II.[15] I have argued elsewhere that mutual self-mediation, friendship, and discernment are the methodological presuppositions in the church's relations *ad extra* going forward from the council. However, to say that this recognition occurs does not mean that it has been received, or that the effects of it have been implemented in the life of the church. Given that there were no condemnations at Vatican II, we might surmise that a new method for engaging the other is called for, one that invokes discernment of the fruits of the Spirit and an ecclesiology (the "church as friend") to support such an endeavour.[16]

Let us try to specify how theology functions as a mediator between a culture and a religion based on Lonergan's notion of mediation. First, there would be an immediate ("a source, an origin, a ground, a basis") and there would be a mediated ("a result, consequence, outcome, insofar as it arises in a field of radiation, expansion, influence, insofar as it manifests, expresses, reveals, the basis") (*CWL* 6, 13). The immediate is the religious tradition as engaged, understood, appropriated by a theologian or group of theologians committed to that tradition. The mediation via the theologian(s) would be to promote an understanding of the religious tradition to a culture. In the past this would be known as apologetics. However, the "mutual" in mutual self-mediation implies that the process is to be explicitly a two-way street, a sincere dialogue.

16   The Wisdom of Order

Theologians encounter attitudes, meanings, and values in the culture(s) through listening. Some of these attitudes, meanings, and values will help enrich their understanding of the faith, and some of them will challenge the church; some of the theologians may discern a need to challenge the culture, and some attitudes, meanings, and values will signal areas of development and lack of development in the culture. A painful, if necessary, aspect of this historical mediation comes about when the advance of theology, through this mutual interaction, brings about a demythologization of current religious conceptions. Galileo's science challenged the literal interpretation of the biblical accounts of creation during his time. It took the official church five hundred years to forgive him.

In contrast, in the mediation of culture to a religion, the culture is the immediate and its effects are mediated in the theology in an engagement with the religious tradition. Theologians would also mediate an understanding of the religious tradition, the mysteries of the faith, to their own faith community. In this encounter, there will be differences between the religion and the culture that complement and enrich a mutual understanding, there will be differences that challenge the church to change, there will be differences that call for the church to prophetically challenge the culture to change, and there will be differences in areas where the culture has outgrown the religion or the religion has outgrown the culture. For example, the Catholic Church no longer has the same commitment to establishing hospitals it once had in economically developed countries, since government and private industries have taken over that ministry once pioneered by the church. Doran invokes the example of John Courtney Murray, who championed the teaching on religious liberty of Vatican II.[17] In dialoguing with a key aspect of his culture, influenced as he was by democratic principles of freedom, Murray brought the church to a new teaching exemplified in Vatican II's Declaration on Religious Freedom, *Dignitatis humanae*. It was that document that prompted people to say of Vatican II that it was the end of the Constantinian era of the church. Among other things, *Dignitatis humanae* rejects forced or coerced conversions to Christianity.[18]

Of course, not everyone was delighted with *Dignitatis humanae* at Vatican II. It prompted Bishop Lefebvre and his entourage to leave the church – an exercise of their own religious freedom, paradoxically dependent upon the very principles of the declaration they rejected. In any event, Murray is an interesting case because his work demonstrates a theologian's listening to a culture, gleaning something of important value, and establishing a theological doctrine based on that value that in turn is received into ecclesiastical doctrine.

The mutual self-mediation of diverse self-mediating communities with one another presumes developments, transpositions, and paradigm shifts in self-understanding. In this mutual self-mediation, it is not only theology that develops; culture too is always undergoing change through the dynamism of progress, decline, and the elevation of grace. If listening is to be integrated into a method in theology, it will go hand-in-hand with discernment as a methodological principle. From the church's point of view, it may require, from time to time, a methodological kenosis in order to empty itself of the vestiges of the past that give way to transpositions of ever-changing paradigm shifts.[19] In what ways is the church still in need of demythologization? Such is the perennial import of the tag *ecclesia semper reformanda*.

An Empirical Notion of Culture

Related to the previous discussion – and comprising a significant paradigm shift for theology – is what Lonergan calls the movement from a classicist notion of culture to an empirical notion of culture. This shift, along with the recognition of mutual self-mediation, combine to complexify and enrich theology in our era. Among other things, this shift to an empirical method undergirds the rise in contextual theologies with its various hermeneutic starting points. Conversely, this empirical turn reveals the degree to which theology, without surrendering its underpinning truth claims, is always to some degree contextual.

From the standpoint of the empirical notion of culture, culture is "the set of meanings and values that informs a way of life" (3). As an analogy, one can think of the shift to the empirical as *the hand* while the various contextual approaches are *the fingers*. This is admittedly a rough analogy given the numerous intersectional starting points in contemporary theological reflection. But what brought this paradigm shift about was the emergence of scientific method with an empirical starting point, the emergence of historical consciousness along with history as a field of academic study, and the emergence of anthropology as a social science.

How might one date this paradigm shift to an empirical notion of culture? An argument can be made that it begins about the same time Lonergan identities as when theology fell behind the times, a falling behind that lasted until the eve of Vatican II. Lonergan confidently provides a specific year: 1680. In his essay "Theology in Its New Context" (*CWL* 13, 48–59),[20] Lonergan identifies three reasons for choosing this date: (1) Paul Hazard places this as the beginning of the Enlightenment, (2) Herbert Butterfield chooses the same year as the birth of modern science, and (3) Yves Congar places the birth of dogmatic theology in this year. In this third development, theology became strictly deductive, invoking Aristotelian logic as a key part of its methodology. It also became defensive in its posture towards a world increasingly critical of Christianity and Roman Catholicism in particular. As science was moving out of the Aristotelian paradigm, it became more inductive, that is, beginning with the empirical, raising questions, formulating hypotheses, experimenting in order to corroborate the hypothesis, and identifying or corroborating laws as a result of those studies. One of the ways theology fell behind the times was in its attempt to go in the reverse direction to that of modern scientific induction by adopting a form of logical deduction that modern science had moved beyond. Melchior Cano's *De locis theologicis* (1562) attempted to be scientific, to be sure, but it was an attempt based on an Aristotelian science that was overwhelmingly deductive, an approach that the emerging notion of modern science was reversing by replacing the deductive method with an empirical starting point and inductive one.

In keeping with this date of 1680, and independent of Lonergan's analysis, it is interesting to note that Marvin Harris argues that the social science of anthropology has its origins in the publication of John Locke's *An Essay on Human Understanding*, which, published in 1689, is in close historical proximity to 1680.[21] In his *Essay*, Locke argued that the mind is essentially a blank slate that socialization, education, and formation subsequently fill in. This brought tremendous attention to how culture is learned, a process commonly known as *enculturation*.

While highly influential, Locke's work contains an epistemological oversight because it cannot account for original and creative insights, of which the mind is capable. For example, on Locke's own presuppositions, someone would have to teach Locke that the mind was a blank slate because he would have been incapable of forming the original insight about the blank slate of his own mind in the first place – incapable as the mind is, at least according to him, of original insights. But performative contradictions aside, Locke's influence has been vast and enduring. The volume and popularity of culture studies discourse today is a legacy of his tome, given that we are formed by cultures. Moreover, one could argue that even the empirical notion of culture is part of that legacy, insofar as the social sciences followed the physical sciences by an insistence upon on an empirical starting point. The shift from the classicist notion of culture to an empirical one led naturally to the emergence of contextual theologies, some of the principal ones being liberationist, feminist, African, and Asian, to name a few. But even these can be almost endlessly subdivided, since, just like the empirical notion of culture, there are as many potential contextual theological starting points and intersections as there are historical communities with various experiences.

A corollary to this empirical starting point is that *experience* becomes a source for theology. George Fox (1624–1691), the founder of Quakerism, brought attention to the "Inner Light" of religious experience, an emphasis that threatened the world view of the externally focused Puritans of New England and prompted the scapegoating of converts to Quakerism such as Mary Dyer. Charles Wesley (1707–88), the founder of Methodism, elaborated his famous "quadrilateral" that emphasized scripture, tradition, reason, and *experience*. Friedrich Schleiermacher (1768–1834) situated experience at the heart of his theology as *Gefühl*, the feeling of absolute dependence – at once an experience, existential condition, and awareness of some ultimate transcendent value.

In contrast to the empirical, inductive notion of culture, the classicist notion of culture was normative, permanent, universal, stable, idealistic, unchanging, and ahistorical. It held one culture to be *the* "culture," or "civilized," and labelled others as "barbarian" or "savage." The distinction between *high culture* and *low culture* is also one of its effects. One was "cultured" to the extent that one was schooled and formed in this classicist (European) mentality. To become a Christian was to become European since the two were not differentiated (*CWL* 13, 119, 197). The effects of this colonial mentality on Indigenous peoples are well documented.[22]

Growing up before Vatican II and amidst the cultural revolutions of the mid-1900s, Lonergan himself was formed in this classicist notion of culture; his awareness of and liberation from that mentality began with his reading of Christopher Dawson's *The Age of the Gods* (*CWL* 13, 222). The content of Dawson's book is not as important as the fact that it introduced Lonergan to the idea of history as a key component to the study of theology. Theology in a classicist mentality is ahistorical. By contrast, the discovery of the importance of history for theology was an ongoing interest of Lonergan's throughout his life, so much so that he claimed that his entire life project was "introducing history into Catholic theology."[23]

Nevertheless, Lonergan is careful neither to demonize the classicist notion of culture nor to glorify the empirical one. They both have their limitations, although he is clear that the empirical notion of culture is here to stay, and clinging to the classicist notion of culture is obstructionist to the development of theology in our era. That said, one must keep in mind that the classicist mentality still exists in degrees, like radioactivity. Some contexts possess it in greater quantities than others. In Roman Catholic circles, it exists in certain segments of the community especially as it pertains to ecclesiology or the theology of church. In previous work, I have labelled this tendency *classicist ecclesiology*, insofar as the attitude flows from a belief that the church is permanent, unchanging, and therefore unaffected by history.

Finally, linked to the eclipse of the classicist notion of culture is the discovery of historical consciousness and historical scholarship. There are different senses of history in Lonergan's work. One can distinguish in his work (1) *history as scholarship*, as represented in the functional specialty *history*, which he outlines in two chapters in *Method in Theology*; (2) *a philosophy of history* as outlined in the stages of meaning (common sense, theory and interiority); and (3) *a theology of history* that includes the threefold dynamic of progress, decline, and redemption. This conception of a theology of history was with him from early on in his career to his later essays.[24]

Lonergan's life work on method is an attempt to reckon with the turn to experience and inductive method bought about by the emergence of modern science, the philosophical turn to the subject, and the rise of historical consciousness and historical scholarship. In a word, these are all significant developments. Vatican II represented the church's beginning to come to terms with these movements in an unprecedented manner, so much so that Lonergan declares: "The meaning of Vatican II was the acknowledgement of history."[25] This acknowledgment of history would naturally lead to an emphasis on foundational theology; accordingly, as we noted in the introduction, Vatican II specifically called for work in this area, and the implementation in ecclesiastical studies of a new, revised course dedicated to it. The recognition of historical consciousness substituted out the classicist construal of foundational theology for an inductive one – one that must take the changed philosophical context, among other things, into account. The same inductive approach also brought with it an ever-expanding body of knowledge, and with it, increasing differentiation and specialization. Without some unifying principle, a fragmentation of knowledge results.

Finally, it goes without saying that such an inductive approach has occasioned theology's taking into account a social history of economic disparities, the scapegoating of the marginalized, and the preferential option for the poor, which have come to the fore in Catholic social teaching.[26]

The empirical notion of culture has brought with it its own set of challenges and difficulties. The introduction of history into theology occasions a temptation to relativism. The empirical starting point brings with it a pluralism of intellectual, cultural, and religious perspectives. Among other things, this leads to fluid or hybrid religious identities, further frustrating classicist nostalgia for clearer identity. Moreover, the vast amount of data, knowledge, and specialization that follows from this empirical turn leads to a fragmentation of knowledge – any interdisciplinary theoretical synthesis seems daunting and overwhelming. In response, specialists fall back into the comfort of their own expertise. The danger with this tendency is for specialists to compartmentalize and consequently "know more and more about less and less" (122). The lack of a basic philosophical method to unify the various specialist methodologies, compounded by the surplus of information, exacerbates this fragmentation of knowledge.

And so, we are left with a legacy of philosophical, ethical, and religious doubt. There is debate among philosophers whether we can know, and, if so, how we actually know. There is debate among ethicists whether the good exists or what constitutes general ethical criteria. There is a secularism that questions the legitimacy of religion, and there is a religious pluralism that raises questions about the legitimacy of any particular religion's truth claims.

Lonergan's entire intellectual project attempts to meet the philosophical pluralism of our time, which he discerns to have three sources: (1) the various linguistic-social-cultural-religious contexts, (2) the various realms of meaning or differentiations of consciousness, and (3) the presence of blocks to authenticity (see 303). Lonergan's endeavour in *Method in Theology* is to ameliorate the fragmentation of knowledge that flows from such compartmentalization. He offers a response to the philosophical/ethical issues in chapter 1 of the text when he outlines his generalized empirical method. The response to religious pluralism occurs in chapter 4, on religion. In any case, the recognition that the mediation of theology between religion and culture is a two-way street and the empirical notion of culture are paradigmatic and necessary methodological considerations in our contemporary situation. Necessary, too, is a recognition that the criteria for navigating these complex times call for personal and communal discernment *a posteriori*, rather than dogmatic certainty *a priori*. And proper discernment requires wisdom. Lonergan's *Method in Theology* is an attempt to bring about a wise ordering for our complex times.

Method Defined

In a sense, Lonergan's call for a movement from a classicist to an empirical notion of culture goes hand in hand with a shift in theological method. This is so, first, because the shift to an empirical notion of culture creates the conditions for a shift in theological method. "When culture is conceived empirically, theology is known to be an ongoing process, and then one writes on its method" (3). Second, although not specifically stated by Lonergan, the deductive process of the classicist mindset is analogous to a deductive methodology, which views method as a set of rules to be followed meticulously. By contrast, contemporary theological method is conceived of as "a framework for collaborative creativity" (3). Modelling itself on developments in modern science, history, scholarship, and philosophy, this method will entail groups of "clusters of operations" that Lonergan conceives of as occurring in eight functional specialties: research, interpretation, history, dialectic, foundations, doctrines, systematics, and communications (praxis). These eight tasks are treated in more detail in the second part of the book. The first part of the book contains five chapters treating "general" topics that have to be "presupposed" in the second part: method, the human good, meaning, religion, and the functional specialties.

A Model?

Before proceeding, Lonergan asks whether what he is presenting is a model, or whether it is more than a model. On the one hand, he is offering a model, not in the sense of "something to be copied or imitated" or a "description of reality or a hypothesis," but in the sense of "an intelligible, interlocking set of terms and relations" helpful for describing or hypothesizing about reality (4). On the other hand, Lonergan offers more than a model in the sense that his claims are verifiable within one's own intentional consciousness. Chapter 1, on method, which we explore next, will present this theory to be corroborated by one's own introspective analysis. Much of the rest of the book is a "prolongation" of the first chapter, and so is subject to the same kind of verifiability.

Finally, Lonergan makes two important qualifications. First, he is addressing not the objects of theology per se, but the operations theologians perform when they are doing theology. An assumption Lonergan is making is that historical and biblical studies would fall under the broader method of theology and are integral to its output. In our current climate, these disciplines have become so autonomous and specialized that Lonergan's proposal may seem too ambitious. However, it has the benefit of getting biblical, historical, and systematic theologians talking to one another, and is therefore worthy of pursuit. Second, he suggests that this method may have use beyond his own context, the Roman Catholic one. He leaves it up to other "communions" to decide whether the method is appropriate for them. We will find out later that he also believes the method has broader interdisciplinary applications.

2 Method

A Third Way

Traditionally, method has been conceived of, fundamentally, in two ways: (1) as something to be learned by observing, imitating, or modelling a master, and (2) as analogous to scientific method. The first is learned performatively and cannot be taught in the classroom as such. One latches on to a mentor or master and simply listens, observes, imitates, and incorporates. But there can be a lack of masters and mentors, and even then, one is not encouraged to reflect on the more basic operations of method. Moreover, such a view of method does not explicitly account for or allow for personal appropriation and creative adaptation. Second, method is viewed as analogous to "science." By this is meant the "natural sciences." This tendency has its roots in Aristotle, who preferred the exactness of mathematics because it did not have to account for the contingency of the external world. Mathematics relies on deduction and the intelligibility inherent in necessity and impossibility to produce exact results. When one moves to empirical observation, one has to account for contingency.

In more recent times, we have seen a preference for science so understood in the distinction between the "hard sciences" (physics, astronomy, chemistry) and the "soft sciences" (anthropology, psychology, sociology). In *Insight* Lonergan refers to "laws," understood in the classically "scientific" sense as "classical laws." These predominate in the former. He also refers to statistical laws, often invoked by the social sciences. However, for him "soft science" is a pejorative term that discounts the legitimate intelligibility of statistical laws (*CWL* 3, chaps. 3–5). A mechanist-determinist tries to construe world processes based entirely on classical laws. The pejorative labelling of the social sciences, which rely on statistical laws, as "soft science" is a residual effect of a mechanistic bias, one unfortunately kept alive by common priorities in the allotment of research funding that tend to favour projects that can yield exact results. In reality, statistical laws admit of a different kind of intelligibility than classical laws. To be useful in the "real world," mathematics has to be applied in engineering and the applied sciences. In contrast, classical science deals in observation, hypotheses, and experimentation. Predictability as the corroboration of hypotheses is the gold standard for classical science. The closer the observation and experimentation come to corroborating the hypothesis, the closer one comes to verifying laws. The exactness and predictability of classical science indicate that scientists have discovered classical laws (e.g., gravitation). But even then, Galileo's law of falling bodies holds only in a vacuum, or if "all things are equal." In other words, it holds only if there are no contingencies in the external world that would interfere. Those contingencies are not always determined by classical laws, but rather are the product of statistical laws (e.g., contingencies foreseen by the science of meteorology).

The more predictable the outcome of scientific experimentation, as in the case of classical science, the less contingency one must take into account. The more contingency one has to take into account, the more one is likely dealing with statistical laws. But there is an added complexity when social scientists start to explore human nature. For the human being is not just a compound of classical and statistical laws, but also of developmental laws, subject further to the self-constitution of personal freedom. In a word, much of human behaviour is unpredictable because human beings do not always act attentively, intelligently, reasonably, responsibly, and lovingly.

A third way to approach method is needed that avoids the strict analogy of the natural sciences and its attempt to place all fields of knowledge in a preferential hierarchical order. Lonergan will attempt to articulate this third way by going "behind the procedures of the natural sciences to something both more general and more fundamental, namely the procedures of the human mind" (8). This basic pattern of operations he will call *transcendental method*, or generalized empirical method. It is the generalized or universal method behind every kind of inquiry of which the human mind is capable.

Method

"A method is a normative pattern of recurrent and related operations yielding cumulative and progressive results" (8). This definition is general. It applies to all methods of human inquiry, not only mathematics, the natural and human sciences, and all fields of application, but also our everyday encounters with human beings, in practical matters and in exercises of creativity. This definition of method requires distinct operations, each set related to one another in a proper recurrent pattern. However, the recurrence is not simply for the sake of repetition: there is an accumulation and progression of knowledge and wisdom that results (8). *Pace* our above problematization, the scientific method in the natural sciences provides one of the clearest examples of this dynamic, and Lonergan expounds upon this method in more detail. While there are operations specific to science (inquiry, observation, experimentation, hypothesis, etc.), Lonergan seeks to identify more generally the pattern of operations behind those scientific operations.

Method is not a set of rules to follow blindly, for this approach cannot allow for discoveries, syntheses, and the accumulation of knowledge. Still, the notion of method Lonergan anticipates will identify the pattern of operations from which rules can be derived. Nor are the patterns to be logical operations, even though logic has its place: some of the operations lie outside of logical operations (e.g., inquiry, observation, and discovery). Lonergan makes the astute observation that modern science has grouped together logical and non-logical operations. The former sort tends to "consolidate what has been achieved"; the latter keeps the process open to further discovery. Altogether, the scientific method is "open, ongoing, progressive, and cumulative." This is in contrast to Aristotelian science, which focused on the "necessary and the immutable," and the Hegelian dialectical approach that was "enclosed in a complete [rationalist] system" (10).

Let us identify the basic pattern of what Lonergan calls *transcendental method*, which is his basic philosophy of interior consciousness. There are four basic levels or groups of operations:

- *Experiencing (presentations)*:[1] seeing, hearing, touching, smelling, tasting
- *Understanding*: inquiring, imagining, understanding (insight), conceiving, formulating
- *Judging*: reflecting, marshalling and weighing the evidence, (reflective insight) judging
- *Deciding*: deliberating, evaluating, deciding, acting (*MT*, 10)

In order to proceed, Lonergan admonishes the reader to become familiar with his terminology as regards the basic pattern. Moreover, he encourages the reader to verify this basic pattern in his or her own conscious experience. The unwillingness to do this will render the study as useless as a lecture on colour to someone who is blind (11).

At this point I would make two observations. First, there has been a tendency for students and scholars to resist studying Lonergan because they do not want to learn his technical vocabulary and become accustomed to his writing style. To some extent I can sympathize with this attitude in that trying to understand his thought takes a certain amount of effort and commitment. However, I think it can become an excuse either to avoid or to dismiss the value of his contribution. In fact, students and scholars have no problem learning the language of those philosophers and theologians who are in vogue, such as Heidegger's *Dasein* or Levinas's *illeity*. Indeed, it may take a pope to see the value in Lonergan's thought for it to gain a wider significance. But Lonergan scholars are partly to blame for the antipathy towards his thought. Their cliquishness, tendency to engage in excessive and abstruse conceptualizing, and cavalier enthusiasm at times alienate the curious and further justify antagonists of his thought. Full disclosure: I have been guilty of cavalier enthusiasm myself, especially in the early days after my discovery of his thought.

My second observation is more to Lonergan's point. One must (1) learn the vocabulary and concepts Lonergan espouses, and (2) then verify them in one's own experience. To perform these two operations correlates with the second and third levels of his cognitional theory: *understanding* and *judgment*, respectively. First, one must understand what the method is, and then one should verify it in one's own conscious operations of intentional consciousness. This means that one does not have to take Lonergan's word for it: there is no question of coercing one to consent. It can only be verified in one's own experience. Of course, if one does not verify it, one may live in a performative self-contradiction; but one would not be alone in that condition. It is a common mistake made my many a scientist and philosopher who denies the possibility of knowing, and yet lives as if their very denial of truth did not apply to their own truth claims.

Back to the four sets (levels) of operations. Lonergan makes seven points regarding this philosophical method. First, he states that the operations as listed earlier are transitive. Generally, this means that, grammatically, they have the *–ing* ending. More important is the psychological sense of the operations by which a conscious subject becomes aware of an "object." The objects are proportionate to the respective operations: for example, sounds are proportionate to hearing, images to seeing, and so on. Each of the operations is intentional in that each intends an object proportionate to the specific operation (e.g., hearing does not intend visual images: it intends sounds).

Second, the list of operations implies both grammatically and psychologically a conscious subject. A conscious subject is one who sees, hears, thinks, speaks, and so on. This subject is conscious through these operations. When there are no operations operating, the subject is asleep or unconscious. Moreover, the subject is conscious in a qualitatively different way with respect to the different operations. While it is true that the subject experiences herself or himself as operating, this experience is not per se an additional operation. This "experiencing is not intending but being conscious" (12). Waking consciousness immediately issues in the intrinsic intentional operations that make one more fully conscious as one rises out of bed.

This operating subject is also self-present: "Just as operations by their intentionality make objects present to the subject, so also by consciousness they make the operating subject present" to herself or himself (12). An object may be present to a subject, but that kind of presence is different from the presence of the subject to her or his seeing, hearing, judging, and so on. The subject is present to herself or himself through the operations, and is also able to determine the level of attention she or he gives to an object as attended to, be it partial or full attention.

Lonergan distinguishes a broader notion of experience from his technical philosophical use of the term. There is the broad sense of experience associated with a person of knowledge and practical wisdom. In this sense, experience "includes everything that is in the person's development." The narrower sense of experience refers to the "sense of the data ... the givenness that constitutes the data, which is the presupposition of the act of understanding" (*CWL* 13, 185–6).

In *The Ontological and Psychological Constitution of Christ*, Lonergan is even more nuanced in his analysis of consciousness and experience. Under the formality of the experienced (*sub ratione experti*), one can distinguish interior and exterior experience. Exterior experience refers to the objects presented to consciousness as apprehended through the five senses. Interior experience refers to the unstructured awareness of the subject as present to objects, and the subject present to her or his operations. Consciousness "is not just any awareness of oneself and one's acts, but only that awareness that is preliminary and unstructured."[2] While it is true that the subject experiences herself or himself as operating, this experience is not per se an additional operation. This "experiencing is not intending but being conscious" (*CWL* 14, 12).

Third, by introspection Lonergan does not mean taking an inward gaze at oneself as if consciousness were an operation itself. This myth of inward inspection rests on the analogy of knowing as ocular vision. Through vision alone one does not understand; rather, one simply sees. The contents of that vision and the images apprehended may become the basis for inquiry and knowledge. The default philosophical mistake in Western history is to think that knowing is like looking – that the real is to be apprehended by gazing upon the "already-out-there-now," that human knowing is simply "animal knowing."

By "introspection," Lonergan means to make the operations of consciousness the object of one's intellectual inquiry, adverting to them in one's experience, relating them to one another in one's understanding, and affirming that such operations occur in a judgment (the self-affirmation of the knower). In a word, it is to move from the data of sense to the data of consciousness, subjecting the conscious operations themselves to inquiry, insight, and judgment. This is what the reader is encouraged to do in order to verify the basic method for all human inquiry and discovery. He describes the process in *CWL 7* as follows:

> First, consciousness is not just any awareness of oneself and one's acts, but only that awareness that is preliminary and unstructured. For example, by way of the first operation of the intellect you acquire an awareness of yourself when you grasp and define what a human being is; and through the same operation of the intellect you come to an awareness of your own acts when you grasp and define what is meant by seeing, understanding, judging, willing, desiring, fearing, enjoying, grieving, and so on. Similarly, through the second operation of the intellect you come to an awareness of yourself and your acts in making the judgment that you are a human being, that you see, that you understand, and so forth. All this knowledge comes through intellectual inquiry, and so is not at all what we have referred to as consciousness. For consciousness is prior to intellectual inquiry and, like exterior experience, needs to be completed by it. (161)

Fourth, as indicated earlier in the list of the four basic groups of operations (p. 25), these various groups of operations are to be distinguished as distinct "levels." There are four levels in the waking state. But prior to waking, consciousness during sleep is "fragmentary and incoherent." Lonergan was quite taken with the phenomenologist Ludwig Binswanger's theory of dreams, although he does not cite him at this point. Binswanger distinguished dreams of the middle of the night and dreams closer to waking consciousness.[3] Late-night dreams reflected the physiology of the body in its regulatory processes. Those dreams closer to waking consciousness begin to anticipate the matters at hand in the subject's day. Whether science has corroborated Binswanger's theory is beside the point; what Lonergan focused on was the fact that this theory corroborated his own beliefs about intentional consciousness. It would make sense for Lonergan that waking consciousness would, in a rudimentary way, anticipate the objects of the day. The impulse of our intentional intellectual, rational, and deliberative consciousness is operative even before we rise. Once awake, however, there are four basic types of consciousness:

> There is the *empirical* level, on which we sense, perceive, imagine, feel, speak, move. There is an *intellectual* level, on which we inquire, come to understand, express what we have understood, work out the presuppositions and implications of our expression. There is the *rational* level, on which we reflect, marshal the evidence, pass judgment on the truth or falsity, certainty or probability, of a statement. There is the *responsible* level, on which we are concerned with ourselves, our own operations, our goals, and so deliberate about possible courses of action, evaluate them, decide and carry out our decisions. (13)

The quality of consciousness on each of these levels is different. Each "expands" and builds upon the prior. As experience leads to inquiry and insight, understanding gives way to the judgment of what really is the case, and deliberation engages what is to be done with the facts discovered. Each level provides a fuller consciousness as one reaches deliberation. In deliberation, one has reached the fully self-conscious act of self-understanding.[4] For here, one not only makes decisions, but constitutes oneself as a moral being through those decisions.[5] At this fourth level, "we emerge as persons, meet one another in a common concern for values, seek to abolish the organization of human living on the basis of competing egoisms and to replace it by an organization on the basis of [human beings'] perceptiveness and intelligence ... reasonableness, and ... responsible exercise of freedom" (14). In fact, the articulation of this fourth level, which in Lonergan's systematics of the Trinity he calls an "existential act of autonomy," is quite important in Lonergan's theoretical development.[6] The Election as discussed in St. Ignatius's second week of the *Spiritual Exercises* would have brought home to him the self-constitution in one's act of freedom. It will also come into play when we examine the possibility of a fifth level – being in love.

Fifth, the different groups of operations in intentional consciousness yield different modes of intending. For example, the data of sense are linked directly to the five senses and intentionality at this level is "selective" rather than "creative" (14). We could not possibly advert to all of the sense data that come into our frame of reference during the day, so we must be selective. In many ways, this happens automatically by virtue of our familiarity with our environment, our interests (conation), and other factors. But our inquiring minds can be stirred by the data of sense and ask questions about that experience. For example, at one point ancient inquirers wondered why the moon appears in different shapes on different nights. The shapes were described, and patterns identified. From this came the discovery of the phases of the moon, and thence the conclusion of its sphericity.[7]

But the imagination can also provide data, and so there are also data of consciousness. When we imagine a unicorn, we advert to the data of our consciousness. The intentionality of the imagination can be "representative or creative." It is representative when an artist attempts to depict a tree. It is creative when one creates imaginary narratives and explores different possibilities over and above reality.

The intentionality of insight is not the "data of sense," nor the construction of the imagination, but the "intelligible organization," the grasp of the unity in the data or in the relations among the data that "may or may not be relevant to the data" (14). By contrast, conception intends the content of the insight and the "image as essential to the occurrence of the insight," so that it intends the "concrete being" expressed abstractly (14).

Two other kinds of intending are the categorial and the transcendental. Categories are those "determinations" that possess "limited denotation" and "cultural variation." By contrast, transcendentals are "unrestricted in denotation," "comprehensive in connotation," and "invariant over cultural change." Transcendentals "are contained in questions prior to answers" (15). How are we to understand this statement? His distinction is novel in that he distinguishes the transcendental concepts from transcendental notions. The concepts are the objectifications of the intending at each level of intentional consciousness. The objectification of the intending consciousness at the level of understanding ("What is it?") is the intelligible; at the third level, judgment ("Is it so?"), it is truth and reality; and at the fourth level, decision ("Is it valuable?" or "What should I do?"), it is value or the truly good. The concepts are often misinterpreted, especially given their generality and abstraction. Therefore, Lonergan emphasizes the transcendental notions. They are *a priori* in the sense that when I ask a question, the question as it arises genuinely from my inquiring spirit includes the form of the answer. In the question "What is it?" is included the anticipation of intelligibility. In the question "Is it so?" is included the anticipation of the true and the real. In the questions "Is it valuable?"

or "What should I do?" is included the anticipation of true value – or, in other words, the right thing to do.

Constitutive of our conscious intentionality, the transcendental notions form the dynamism of our knowing and doing by moving us beyond experience to understanding, beyond understanding to judgment, and beyond judgment to decision and action. To go against this dynamism or obstruct it in any way is to "obscure" the dynamism of true knowing and right action (15).

Sixth, Lonergan distinguishes between elementary and compound intending (knowing) and their corresponding objects. Elementary knowing pertains to individual operations such as seeing, hearing, understanding, and the like. The corresponding objects, or what is intended in elementary knowing, pertain to what is seen, heard, understood, and the like, respectively. Compound knowing is the combination of several elementary components of knowing into a single compound (experience, understanding, and judgment). There is a further element of decision (action) that involves choosing in accordance with what one knows, or choosing true value. In reality, we only need to be concerned with two compounds: (1) that which involves *knowing* is a compound of experience, understanding, and judgment,[8] and (2) that which involves right *doing* is a compound of experience, understanding, judgment, and decision.

Our knowing and doing is not a willy-nilly fragmentation of elements: through the transcendental notions we intend the unknown and the truly good. The compounding of the elements is the work of the transcendental notions that orient us with insatiable curiosity to the mysterious unknown. When the compound is unobstructed by ignorance, error, negligence, or malice,[9] what is experienced is the same as what is understood, what is judged to be true, and what is judged to be truly valuable (15–16).

Seventh, all of these elementary and compound aspects of knowing and doing are one "single thrust, the eros of the human spirit" (16). This eros manifests itself in the transcendental notions, and Lonergan suggests these notions can ground a fourfold differentiation of consciousness: "a moral pursuit of goodness, a philosophic pursuit of truth, a scientific pursuit of understanding, an artistic pursuit of beauty" (16).

Finally, "the basic pattern of conscious and intentional operations is dynamic" (17). Lonergan notes it is materially dynamic in the way dance movements or patterns of music are materially dynamic. This is an interesting point in itself, since the term "levels" has its own connotation of associated images; but Lonergan here implies dance and music as possible alternative images.

32   The Wisdom of Order

The pattern is also formally dynamic in that the various levels of groups of operations (experience, understanding, judgment, and decision) build upon one another (understanding builds upon experience, judgment builds upon experience and understanding, etc.). Finally, this "doubly dynamic pattern" is insatiable and oriented ultimately towards the knowledge of everything about everything.[10]

Excursus on Transcendental Beauty

The editors of the *Collected Works* edition of *Method in Theology* include a footnote from archival material that addresses the question of transcendental beauty (16–17n10). The question itself was not on Lonergan's radar throughout his career. He was mainly concerned with the transcendentals of intelligibility (unity), goodness, and truth. Moreover, his shift from the transcendental as object (transcendental concepts) to the transcendental intentionality of the subject (transcendental notions implied in the questions) makes the question of beauty more complicated. This author has laboured to understand Lonergan's cryptic, unprepared comments about beauty in a book on the topic.[11] It is encouraging that Lonergan does not hesitate to claim that beauty is a transcendental; but the way he sets up the transcendental notions in *Method* make it difficult to understand how he might explicate the matter. Let us look at his archival statements on beauty more closely.

The way Lonergan sets up a discussion of the transcendental notions as implied in the questions for understanding (intending the intelligible), questions for reflection (intending the true [reality, existence]), and questions for deliberation (intending the good) suggests that beauty as a transcendental would be implied in a question. Perhaps the question would be "Is it beautiful?" But when we consider the language, "a moral pursuit of goodness, a philosophic pursuit of truth, a scientific pursuit of understanding (intelligibility), an artistic pursuit of beauty" (16) we get a clue where Lonergan situates beauty. That is, if we follow him here in terms of the levels of intentional consciousness, we see him situating goodness with the fourth level, decision; truth with the third level, judgment; and intelligibility with the second level, understanding. Is he then implying that the (artistic) pursuit of beauty is on the first level, experience (presentations)? To the extent that he might be, the matter is complicated, first, because at the first level the goal is simply to be attentive to the relevant data of sense and/or consciousness. There are no questions per se that would entail a transcendental notion of beauty. Second, the phrase "the artistic pursuit of beauty" would have to reckon with the fact that beauty has essentially been removed as an aesthetic category in modern thinking on aesthetics. Third, beauty as a transcendental, as he characterizes it here, insofar as it pertains to the first level, would be an aesthetic category rather than a philosophical notion. As a transcendental, beauty would need to be a philosophical notion broadly conceived of as beauty proportionate to existence. If something exists, there is a beauty proportionate to its existence per se. Aesthetic beauty provides an analogy for philosophical beauty, but the latter is more generally conceived of and gives rise to the aesthetic.

Now let us look at Lonergan's comments when he is directly put the question about whether beauty is a transcendental. There are really two passages in Lonergan's corpus, provided below. *CWL* 14 includes only one, from the Dublin lectures (16n10):

1. **From the Dublin Q&A Method in Theology lectures (1971):**

    Question 5: Would you consider the Beautiful as a transcendental? If so, is it distinct from the other transcendentals, or included in one of the others? Further, if it is a transcendental, how does it fit into a correlation with the four-level structure of consciousness?

    Lonergan: The Beautiful is a *different sort of transcendental* [emphasis added]. It is concrete. It is not universal, unlimited in denotation. There are ugly things. It is, as it were, a total response of the person to an object. The other transcendentals are what articulate the type of knowing that is mediated by meaning, by words and so on. Beauty is something that evokes a response from the whole person – it may be through meanings, as in poetry or drama, but it may be apart from meanings in any ordinary sense. It is a type of meaning of its own kind. We will have more to say about this kind of meaning in our third chapter, which is a rather long one.

    Question 36: Would you care to add anything to what you have said about the Beautiful as a transcendental?

    Lonergan: *It is a transcendental, but of a different kind* [emphasis added]. The transcendentals that we have been discussing arise from the differentiations of consciousness. For the Hebrew, truth was fidelity – it was on the fourth level. The Greeks, with their notion of wisdom and *epistémé*, *nous*, and so on, worked out a search for truth as such – that was their *philosophia*. So truth ceased to be fidelity and became something intellectualist. Modern science is concerned with an ongoing process of increasing understanding. The transcendentals I am talking about become clear in so far as that process of differentiation of consciousness occurs. You move from the whole man, with truth just part of his goodness – "doing the truth" – to truth as something cognitional. Modern science moves from cognitional truth to intelligibility. It does not know the truth: it approximates to the truth by an ever-increasing supply of insights. So you have your distinction between intelligibility, truth and reality, and moral goodness. The response of the aesthete to beauty is a response of the total person, without any analysis of his subjectivity. Therefore, it is in a different order. If you want to give it the name "transcendental," alright, but it is not the same sort of thing as the transcendentals that we have been talking about.[12]

2. From the Regis College Method in Theology Institute (1969)

In a question put forth to Lonergan about transcendental beauty he replied:

> Beauty as a transcendental, yes. But it's in terms of developing consciousness, and consciousness at a level in which the higher reaches, the higher concerns, such as truth, reality, value are apprehended through the sensible and are, as it were, a sort of plus to the harmony, the unity, the balance, and so on, that is found in the sensible or the denial of them. The pure desire to know: that is the transcendentals generally or the first one and then moving on to the second and then moving on to the third. Really, that desire is value as opposed to satisfaction – that is what makes it pure. To know value you have to know reality; and to know reality you have to know truth; to know truth you have to grasp intelligibility; and to grasp intelligibility you have to attend to the data; and so it is all one thrust. Beauty is self-transcendence expressed through the sensible ... it is the whole put together.[13]

From these informal comments from Lonergan we can glean several points:

1. Beauty is a transcendental but of a different kind. It is not animated by questions like the other transcendental notions. It also does not seem to be bound up with an increasing differentiation of consciousness. Beauty is not "universal" or "unlimited" (unrestricted) in denotation. This is perplexing, because the idea of a transcendental is that it be general and unrestricted in its predicability. Moreover, Lonergan does not answer the question whether the experience of the subject wholly engrossed in a "beautiful" object is itself a universal experience or an aesthetic one, and if it is an aesthetic experience, how it is related to a philosophical or ontological notion of beauty.

2. Beauty focuses on the response of the whole person to an object, "without any analysis of his subjectivity." This suggests the person may be engrossed in the beautiful object but not inquiring or asking questions or reflecting on the response. This would be why Lonergan places it on the first level, experience, because it is pre-reflective.
3. Beauty is also the thrust of the subject as attending to the data, grasping intelligibility, judging the true and real, and choosing true value. It is the "plus" to this wholly intentional dynamic orientation of the inquiring subject.

The bottom line: it seems Lonergan wanted to acknowledge that beauty was a transcendental (he says so three times) but did not give it the thought required to work out the fuller implications of this perspective. On one hand, he thinks of it as an aesthetic experience prior to the higher levels; on the other, he suggests it is bound up in the subject's intentionality at the higher levels. As noted earlier, in a longer work I try to engage this question of beauty in his philosophy and argue for it more systematically through his entire philosophy of consciousness. I cannot rehearse the entire argument here; but suffice it to say that whereas Bonaventure argued from the side of the object that beauty is a transcendental (the splendour of the transcendentals together), Lonergan indicates that it is a transcendental from the side of the subject (the engagement of the whole subject). Taking Balthasar's critique of the eclipse of beauty as an index on the dramatic situation we find ourselves in, I try to bring Bonaventure and Lonergan together. There is room for more work in this area.[14]

Transcendental Method

Lonergan terms the recurrent pattern of operations (experience, understanding, judgment, and decision) in intentional consciousness *transcendental method*. The term "transcendental" is not to be confused with the Kantian or other uses of the term.[15] He means it in the sense that what it does falls under the purview of a single field or discipline, but is general in its anticipation of all knowledge, inclusive of all fields and disciplines of knowledge. "For transcendental method[16] is the concrete and dynamic unfolding of human attentiveness, intelligence, reasonableness, and responsibility. That unfolding occurs whenever anyone uses his [or her] mind in an appropriate fashion ... Transcendental method will introduce no new resource, it does add considerable light and precision to the performance of ... tasks" (26).

Performatively, everyone is aware of this method in themselves insofar as they attend to their experience, ask questions, and are intelligent in their understanding and responsible in their judgments and decisions. We are not sleepwalkers! Lonergan distinguishes between the "normative pattern immanent in our conscious and intentional operations" from the "objectifications of that pattern in concepts, propositions, words" (21). But what is needed is to make this pattern explicit in one's consciousness and to affirm it as such – in a word, to objectify the pattern in one's conscious intentionality and affirm it as such. This entails taking the four operations and making them the object of one's conscious intentionality. One adverts to one's data of consciousness and one asks the questions: what is the intelligible pattern in my conscious intentionality (experience, understanding, judging, deciding); does this intelligible pattern exist in my own consciousness (judgment); and if so, do or will I act in accordance with this normative pattern of my conscious operations? (18).

No one can validate or affirm these questions for someone else: one must do it for oneself. This makes the world of interiority (the world where I take the data of consciousness as the field of inquiry) distinct from the other worlds of common sense, theory, and religion. In the world of interiority, one can only affirm for oneself, and the pattern of operations cannot be verified in any other manner. Other people can follow suit and search for themselves, but ultimately, they are affirming, or not affirming, the pattern of operations for themselves in their respective consciousness. There is a catch, however: one is certainly "free" *not* to affirm the patterns in one's intentional consciousness in accordance with the natural structure; but then one lives in a performative contradiction. The ramifications for method will have negative residual effects. One's concepts and theories of method will not match those in one's own conscious intentionality.

This pattern of operations also means that the normative pattern of operations is not subject to radical revision (21–2). In order to disprove them, one would have to use the very same operations in order to disprove them and would therefore only validate the existence of the operations. But this does not negate the importance for individuals of affirming the operations for themselves.

Functions of Transcendental Method

Having identified the transcendental method in one's own consciousness, what are the functions of this method? Lonergan concludes the chapter by mentioning twelve functions.

First, there is the normative function of the "transcendental precepts" that guide the patterns of operations towards truth and goodness (22–3).[17]

These are: be attentive (to one's experience), be intelligent (in one's understanding), be reasonable (in one's judgment), and be responsible (in one's decisions).

To be attentive means to advert to one's experience, where the data of sense and the data of consciousness are the condition for the stirring of one's curiosity. But the attentiveness is necessary after inquiry begins as one returns to the data in order to select relevant data pertinent to the questions raised. To miss an important clue would obstruct the insights and hypothesis of the investigator.

To be intelligent means first of all to let the questions arise from within one's natural wonder and curiosity. By contrast, to restrict such questions is *obscurantism* and obstructs the pursuit of truth at the font. It happens frequently in various contexts, but especially in traditional religious contexts: for example, when someone is told not to question something. Biblical fundamentalists refuse to ask certain questions of the Bible, while Catholic fundamentalists refuse to question ecclesial hierarchical authority. Still, giving a free rein to human questioning is easier said than done, especially when it comes to self-reflection. The distinguished psychoanalyst and student of Carl Jung Robert Johnson once stated that he had never had a client in therapy who did not resist his questions at some point.[18] Nevertheless, the specific question for understanding is, "What is it?" The medieval Scholastics called it the *quidditas*, or "whatness," of phenomena. Later philosophers would phrase it in questions about the "nature" of a thing, as in "What is the nature of light?" Questions for understanding aim simply to understand what is the nature and matter of the phenomena under investigation. The Presocratics asked what the nature of the universe is. Thales claimed it was *water*, and Heraclitus said it was *fire*. As we would use the terms today, their questions were more philosophical than scientific. Indeed, our understanding develops as we obtain new information, or as new insights emerge; knowledge accumulates and we raise ever-new questions. Being intelligent means not shutting down questioning in the first place, and not failing to grasp a relevant insight, on one hand, or claiming too much for one's insight or theory, on the other.

Questions for understanding lead to further questions for judgment ("Is it so?"). Reasonableness means not just taking the insights for understanding at face value, but asking the further critical question "Is it so?" It means answering all the relevant questions required in order to answer yes or no in a judgment. Unreasonableness means to make a rash judgment before one has answered all relevant questions, or to refuse to make a judgment when all the relevant questions have been answered.

To be responsible pertains to the proper implementation of knowledge. To know the good is to do the good, if one is responsible. In discerning courses of action, one must consider both short- and long-term effects. To ignore either is to be irresponsible. To believe philosophically that one's freedom and decisions are arbitrary is also irresponsible.

Lonergan summarizes: "The ultimate basis of both transcendental and categorial precepts will be advertence to the difference between attention and inattention, intelligence and stupidity, reasonableness and unreasonableness, responsibility and irresponsibility" (23).

Second, there is a critical function to this basic method. Properly identifying the levels of intentional consciousness in cognitional theory leads to a proper knowledge of reality. The critical function seeks to address the accuracy of the cognitional theory. Conversely, not identifying the levels properly leads to a disjunction between a theoretical account of knowing, on one hand, and the performative operation, on the other. "Hume thought the human mind to be a matter of sense impressions linked together by custom. But Hume's own mind was quite original. Therefore, Hume's own mind was not what he considered it to be" (23). Likewise, Wittgenstein assumed that all language was ordinary meaning, the product of custom; but this cannot account for Wittgenstein's own original insight into the language of ordinary meaning. Is his use of the term "word-game" to be considered ordinary or original?[19] This does not mean that these philosophers should be dismissed because of performative contradictions. On the contrary, they should be mined for the insights they give towards filling out our cognitional theory. Many geniuses end up overemphasizing their insights to the neglect of a broader view.

Lonergan raises an interesting question: why there seems to be a scandal when it comes to agreement on philosophical manners. We take the agreed-upon conclusions of science more readily than we would take an account of how all human beings in general come to know. When we venture into the philosophy of consciousness there is rarely consensus. Still, the power that philosophy has to change our world is greatly – and with grave consequences – underestimated by the modern academy. When Hegel had nearly finished penning his famous *Phänomenologie des Geistes*, Napoleon rode through the city he was living in. The next week, soldiers ransacked his office, as was the custom for a newly conquered region.[20] There is an irony in the fact that Hegel's dialectic as expounded in that freshly completed philosophical treatise would influence the young Marx, whose legacy would conquer more political ground than Napoleon ever did, and for a longer period of time.

Third, whereas the critical function calls forth a validation or correction in a cognitional theory, the dialectical function extends this critique from cognitional theory to epistemology and metaphysics. Here one can genetically trace the various major philosophical achievements in history as each informs what Lonergan calls the basic position (in the theory of knowing – experience, understanding, judgment, decision), and from that basis can criticize those that run counter to it.

This is not just an intellectual enterprise, since, for Lonergan, theological method and theological reflection are built directly upon a proper philosophical foundation. The strength of the latter will be reflected in the former, while a weakness in a theology will be directly traceable to an error in cognitional theory.[21]

Fourth, the systematic function of the basic position enables a deeper understanding of the knowing *and* the known. Objectifying the cognitional operations allows us to identify the terms (the levels and operations of intentional consciousness) and their relations to one another (the pattern of relations between experience, understanding, and judgment). In turn, there is an isomorphism in our knowing. This means that each level of operations has a "known" proportionate to its level. Lonergan here is presuming knowledge of his metaphysics in *Insight*. The language of isomorphism means that (1) the level of experience, prior to insight and judgment, is isomorphic with potency for knowledge, (2) at the level of understanding an "object" is grasped in its intelligible (form), and (3) what is known in a true judgment is *act* (real, existing). Knowing occurs in judgment; what is affirmed is no longer potential or formal, but actual.

Fifth, the basic position offers "continuity without imposing rigidity" (24). On one hand, it is not so rigidly settled on the knowledge of the levels of operations as to prevent further refinement and clarification, and it is not smug enough with the continuity of the structure not to remain radically open. On the other hand, there are limits to the refinement, because the normative outlines of the structure are settled, although this does not preclude what Lonergan calls "minor revisions" and what I have termed "major minor revisions."[22]

Sixth, the acquisition of knowledge involves a transformation of the unknown into a known. Between ignorance and knowledge lies intentionality. This intentionality of cognitional process has a heuristic (anticipatory) function. The intending has a corresponding intended object to be known. This is most simply demonstrated in a question that anticipates an answer; but all cognitional operations anticipate (or intend) a "to-be-known." It is interesting to consider that the nature of our knowing involves a transformation from a prior condition of unknowing to that of the known.

Seventh, a foundational function of the basic position (experience, understanding, judgment, and decision) exists insofar as transcendental method (i.e., the generalized empirical method) grounds all specialized methods. Therefore, the various methods of human inquiry can find their common ground in this transcendental method, which provides the common norms for human inquiry. This, in turn, makes possible interdisciplinary collaboration and the resolution of the problems resulting from specialization.

The seventh point leads naturally to the eighth point: transcendental method is relevant to theology. Just as the former grounds the specialized methods of other disciplines, so it will ground the specialized method of theology. Transcendental method may function differently as it is implemented in various specific disciplines, but its foundation (the human mind) is essentially always the same. As we will see, however, each functional specialty within theology will call for a special emphasis on one of the four precepts mentioned earlier: be attentive, be intelligent, be reasonable, and be responsible. Still, no theologian would aspire to contradict the precepts: to be inattentive, stupid, silly, or irresponsible.

Some may object that the objects of theology do not lie within the "transcendental field," the field of potential natural human inquiry, since they pertain to God. Lonergan's ninth function of transcendental method emphasizes that the transcendental notions ultimately intend to know "everything about everything." They are not abstract notions, but rather concrete, where the intention to know is an orientation to all knowledge, although it is only attained concretely in specific inquiries along the way. The transcendental field is not limited by human knowledge, but by the range of questions human beings can ask. Since we can ask about God, then questions about God lie within the transcendental field. Nothing lies outside of the range of intentional inquiry.

The tenth function of transcendental method adds "no new resource to theology," but it will make explicit a basis for clarity, rigour, and order in the performance of theological tasks. "Theologians always have had minds and always have used them" (26). This of course does not mean that they have always used them intelligently, or have not made mistakes with them. There is a methodological necessity and advantage to making the operations of transcendental method explicit in one's own consciousness. As Lonergan noted in one of his lectures on method: "It is universally relevant because it is always worthwhile to know what one is doing."[23] For example, surgeons are better off if they know what they are doing when they are doing surgery, and why they are doing it. If they cannot distinguish between theory and technique, they risk error and possibly human life.

Transcendental method "offers a key to unified science" (26). Scientists, engineers, and theologians are not different species from one another. They all have human minds. All human intellectual and technological achievements and developments are products of the one human mind. As self-knowledge, self-appropriation, and self-possession become habitually and collectively instantiated in civilization, Lonergan envisions transcendental method will provide the common basis on which the various sciences will be unified – that there will be a common basis in all fields for "common norms, foundations, systematics, and common critical, dialectical, and heuristic procedures" (26). These latter functions refer back to the functions he has already ascribed to transcendental method (in points 1–4 and 6–7; see pp. 22–5).

I would make two notes here about Lonergan's nomenclature, and a point about the unification of the disciplines.

First, notice Lonergan's use of the terms "self-knowledge," "self-appropriation," and "self-possession." The latter two terms would seem to be redundant, since the etymological sense of "appropriate" (from the Latin *appropriare*) is just "to take possession (of a thing)." Self-knowledge means that I have identified the pattern of conscious operations in my own interiority and affirmed them as existing. Self-appropriation means differentiating and habituating that knowledge within myself in order to affect my subsequent interactions and world view. Self-possession involves a slight nuance with respect to the habitualization of this knowledge. It implies a further taking possession of this knowledge in light of the fact that, with the fourth level, decision, I can constitute myself. I can live deliberately in accordance with the transcendental precepts: be attentive, be intelligent, be reasonable, and be responsible.

The second point concerns the unification of the disciplines. The various fields of human knowledge are bounded by the questions asked in each field. Let us take the various branches of the sciences as an example. Subatomic particles are the purview of physics. At some point, the inquiry into those particles becomes an inquiry into compound elements that cease to be questions for physics and become questions for chemistry. When the questions concerning chemical compounds reach their limit, one must move on to the field of biochemistry, and from there to biology. From biology, one moves into sensitive psychology, and so on. The point is that the limiting questions bound the fields of inquiry. At one point, philosophy reaches one of its limiting questions, and the answer must come from theology. In philosophy, the limiting question is, "Why is there something and not nothing?" This question was raised by Heidegger in the twentieth century; but prior to him it was raised by Leibniz in the eighteenth century. Before Leibniz, however, the question was raised by a medieval figure, Siger of Brabant (1240–81). Siger would not have drawn a clear distinction between philosophy and theology, and would have most likely intended it as a theological question. How could it be a theological question? Because the question anticipates a theological answer. One can of course answer, with the nihilist, that there is no reason why there is something and not nothing. But one would then have more explaining to do, and would also have to live one's life as if it were meaningless, and this would go against the fundamental transcendental notions that permeate human intentional consciousness. To answer the question affirmatively would imply a theological conception that has imbued our universe with potential meaning and purpose. This question remains unanswered by the philosopher, and is answered differently by the world's various religions, with their respective individual views on transcendence. Of course, this is not the only bounding question bridging philosophy and theology. There are questions of theodicy and the nature of evil. Philosophy cannot provide a solution to the problem of evil; theology can, and, accordingly, has expressed different solutions in different religions.

But all of this brings us adroitly to Lonergan's twelfth function of transcendental method: namely, that it restores philosophy as the handmaid of theology, although not intrusively. On the contrary, the transcendental method provides the dynamic, open, and stable foundation upon which theology can rest.

"Theologians have minds and they use them" (27). They can also "heighten their consciousness" by making their intentional operations the object of inquiry, and, by so doing, bring to light an important part of theological method. This occurs by asking the three basic questions:

> What am I doing when I am knowing? Why is doing that knowing? What do I know when I do it? The first answer is a cognitional theory. The second is an epistemology. The third is a metaphysics, where, however, the metaphysics is transcendental, and integration of heuristic structures, and not some categorial speculation that reveals that all is water, or matter, or spirit, or process, or what have you. (27)

Transcendental method forms "the anthropological component" for theology. There is still the question of religion to be accounted for, and Lonergan will address this in chapter four of *Method*, "Religion."

However, Lonergan does mention at this point a fourth relevant question, "What do I do with what I know?" This is a question of ethics and practical intelligence that Lonergan treats in chapter 2 of *Method*, which we turn to next.

3 Apprehending and Doing the Good

In chapter 2, "The Human Good," Lonergan presents us with the foundation for his ethics. It is his second explicit attempt at ethics, the first one being chapter 18, "The Possibility of Ethics," in *Insight*. The latter chapter contained a lacuna: it did not account for the roles of feeling and affectivity in ethical deliberation. In this chapter in *Method*, however, Lonergan seeks to integrate feeling and affectivity into the fourth-level decision: ethical and practical deliberation. Moreover, whereas in *Insight* he effected a clear articulation of a judgment of fact and only implied the existence of a judgment of value, in *Method* judgment of value is distinct from judgment of fact.[1] Robert Doran has wondered if the distinct level of decision was affected in Lonergan's lectures on existentialism in 1957,[2] and while there is no explicit evidence at this point, the logic of the hypothesis is not without merit given the existentialists' unabashed emphasis on freedom and the role of decision and action in one's self-constitution.[3] In any case, Lonergan observes his own development:

> In *Insight* the good was the intelligent and reasonable. In *Method* the good is a distinct notion. It is intended in questions for deliberation: Is this worthwhile? Is it truly or only apparently good? It is aspired to in the intentional response of feeling to values. It is known in judgments of value made by a virtuous or authentic person with a good conscience. It is brought about by deciding and living up to one's decisions. Just as intelligence sublates sense, just as reasonableness sublates intelligence, so deliberation sublates and thereby unifies knowing and feeling. (CWL 13, 233)

This is not to say there are no ambiguities surrounding the judgment of value and its role in decision; but these ambiguities will be addressed in due course, and I will suggest my own hypothesis. The disparity between Lonergan's early and later notions of the good has led some to question the value of the earlier version, given its rational approach. But I agree with Doran's view that they represent two different types of decision processes rooted in Ignatian spirituality, in which Lonergan would have been steeped from his Jesuit formation. Doran's view, which I will also discuss, does not force one to choose between the earlier and later ethics, but rather allows one to view them as mutually complementary. Given that there are practical decisions and ethical decisions, practical decisions would be more common in the ethics of *Insight*. All of this will be explored as we exposit Lonergan's notion of the good in *Method*.

The Good

What is the good? Rather than provide us with an abstract definition, Lonergan emphasizes that whatever the good is, it is *concrete*. This means, I should be able to point to something concretely and say, "This x is good": "This apple is good," "This behaviour is good," "It would be good to do x," and the like. In this chapter, Lonergan "aims at assembling various components that enter into the human good" (28). Therefore, he addresses various topics accordingly: skills, feelings, values, beliefs, cooperation, progress, and decline.

The question arises: is Lonergan circling around the issue here by bringing together these various notions, instead of going straight to the point with a judgment of the good? In due course we will find that for Lonergan the content of a "judgment of value" is the good, and it is always concrete. First, however, consider that my making a judgment of value will require a certain set of basic skills; it will involve my feelings and their relations to values. It will be affected by my beliefs and the wider context of cooperation with others, and will be subject to the positive developments of human intelligence and inquiry. Conversely, judgments of value can be negatively affected by bias and moral compromise.

Skills

Lonergan begins with the famous developmental psychologist Jean Piaget (1896–1980). Piaget's work is not only significant for understanding child development, but, for Lonergan, it "goes far beyond the field of educational psychology" (31). There is a link between individual development and the expression of different worlds that forms the basis of culture. But what does Lonergan mean?

For Piaget, the acquisition of skills occurs through analysing elements. New elements emerge through adaptation. Adaptation involves assimilation and adjustment. Assimilation refers to the ease of the exercise of the operations in skill development through repetition. Adjustment refers to the appropriation of those elements through a process of trial and error. Increased adaptation leads to "increasing differentiations of operations." This leads to a mastery of groups of operations and combinations thereof. Piaget's advances in child development theory do not concern us here, but the three things Lonergan takes from Piaget do: *mediation, differentiations,* and *release from the routines of instrumentalized skills.* Some of this will come up in subsequent chapters, so I will simply mention them here. I have already said something about mediation in chapter 1, so I turn to the notion of differentiations. I believe that Piaget influenced Lonergan significantly in this matter, but not with respect to childhood development per se.

What Piaget offered to Lonergan was a further insight into Lonergan's own formulation of patterns of experiences in *Insight* several decades before (see CWL 3, 204–12). Specifically, Piaget gave Lonergan the nomenclature to articulate the habituation of those patterns of experience into differentiated worlds. In *Insight*, Lonergan talks about the intellectual pattern of experience: there is a difference between a child who struggles for an hour to concentrate on mathematics, straining to appropriate the intellectual pattern, and a mathematical physicist, who has learned to live in the intellectual pattern differentiated as a world of theory. More so than patterns of experience, which can be fleeting, differentiations are habituated forms of consciousness reflective of expertise: common sense (practical intelligence as well as dramatic-interpersonal relations), theory, interiority, and religious-mystical experience (3).

This link between patterns and further differentiations was likely a direct result of Lonergan's encounter with the work of Piaget. When Lonergan taught at the Gregorian University from 1953 to 1965, he would often travel to Canada and the United States during the summers in order to give invited lectures and workshops. Of note are three such engagements that later appeared as volumes of his *Collected Works*: (1) the summer of 1957 lectures on existentialism (Boston), published in *CWL* 18, (2) the summer of 1958 lectures on *Insight* (Halifax), published in *CWL* 5,[4] and (3) the summer of 1959 lectures on the philosophy of education (Cincinnati), published as *CWL* 10.[5]

It is interesting to note that Piaget and differentiations of consciousness do not appear in the 1957 and 1958 summer lectures (*CWL* 18 and *CWL* 5). However, in the 1959 lectures, Lonergan discusses Piaget, and used the term "differentiation of consciousness."[6] We will have more to say on the differentiations of consciousness in the next chapter on meaning; but for now it is reasonable speculation that Piaget's ideas allowed Lonergan to move beyond simply speaking about various patterns of consciousness to differentiations of consciousness, the primary difference being that the latter reflects the habituation of a specific pattern experience.

Feelings

In the next section, Lonergan addresses feelings and affectivity. Lonergan draws his theory of feelings principally from Max Scheler (1874–1928) and Dietrich von Hildebrand (1889–1977). But one wonders whether John Henry Newman (1801–90) also implicitly influenced Lonergan on this topic. Lonergan had credited Newman's *Grammar of Assent* as influencing the development of his own notion of judgment, which he expands upon in chapters 9 and 10 of *Insight*. In *Grammar*, Newman argues: "The feeling of conscience (being, I repeat, a certain keen sensibility, pleasant or painful, – self-approval and hope, or compunction and fear, – attendant on certain of our actions, which in consequence we call right or wrong) is twofold: – it is a moral sense, and a sense of duty; a judgment of the reason and a magisterial dictate."[7] Newman's reference to a "feeling" of conscience speaks to the crux of what Lonergan is up to in this chapter on the good. Lonergan wants to articulate how human beings are capable of grasping value, and how a decision proceeds from that grasp. Newman distinguishes two moments in one's experience of this process: (1) the moral sense, which would be for Lonergan the apprehension of value, and (2) the sense of duty: the decision or action that flows from the moral sense. Of course, we will nuance this dynamic process further soon; first we will turn specifically to what Lonergan says about feelings.

Just as operations and habits develop, feelings also develop. Lonergan borrows from von Hildebrand the distinction between non-intentional states and their intentional responses. What distinguishes a non-intentional state is that there is no specific object that arouses the feelings in question. I realize I am tired, irritable, or anxious; but there is no object making me feel that way. A non-intentional state has a cause, so that when I realize I am tired, irritable, or anxious, I may immediately ask myself why I feel that way, so that I can remedy the state. By contrast, non-intentional trends have goals, as is clearly exemplified in the cases of hunger, thirst, and sexual discomfort (32n4).

The role of feelings in non-intentional states is that of cause and effect, while with non-intentional trends, the feelings are orientated to goals.

For example, our feeling of anxiety prompts us to ask the cause; our feeling of hunger prompts us to seek food.

When feelings respond directly to objects, we say these responses are *intentional*. "The feeling relates us not just to a cause or an end, but to an object." The feelings "intend" an object on the level of deliberation. "Intentional responses ... answer to what is intended, apprehended, represented." In this way, feelings enable us to live in the world with full vitality and vigor, when our lives might otherwise be "paper thin" (32).

Moreover, feelings respond to objects in two ways: (1) to the agreeable or disagreeable, the satisfying or dissatisfying, and (2) to value.[8] These two responses can interpenetrate, or they can have nothing to do with each other. I can choose a healthy diet and resist eating candy every night, in which case I undergo privation (the dissatisfying) for the sake of the value of health. On the other hand, I may reward myself with candy in moderation, and truly enjoy the choice of health and the satisfying flavour. I can also choose candy every night, in which case I may find it agreeable and satisfying, but at the expense of my health. Hence, agreeable and disagreeable responses are ambiguous because they may be responding to value or they may not. "What is agreeable may very well be what also is a true good. But it also happens that what is a true good may be disagreeable" (32). As we will see, when someone habitually chooses satisfaction over value, Lonergan would say they are in need of moral conversion.

Excursus: Beauty and Intersubjectivity

A short excursus is in order given Lonergan's initial examples of responding to value, especially one of his few references to beauty. The examples he gives of feelings responding to value are: "the ontic value of persons or the qualitative value of beauty, understanding, truth, virtuous acts, noble deeds" (32).[9] It appears that Lonergan is arranging these examples according to the levels of consciousness of chapter 1. Consider the following schema:

Decision: virtuous acts, noble deeds
Judgment: truth
Understanding: understanding
Experience: beauty and the ontic value of a person [?][10]

It seems clear that the examples of virtuous acts/noble deeds, truth, and understanding correlate with the levels of decision, judgment, and understanding, respectively. Less clear is whether we can associate beauty and the ontic value of a person with the level of *experience*, or *presentations* (as Lonergan sometimes called it). While it is impossible to know if associating the latter two values with the first level of experience is what Lonergan had in mind, allow me to elaborate on beauty and the ontic value of a person and why one might associate them with experience.

Beauty. Lonergan's philosophy does not articulate much about beauty. The question of the transcendentality of beauty was put to him at one point and his impromptu reply was that it was a different kind of transcendental than the common ones: unity, truth, goodness, existence.[11] Lonergan does not work out his thoughts on the transcendentality of beauty in any comprehensive way. In his few references to beauty, he oscillates between two unthematized positions. On one hand, he associates beauty with the first level of experience; on the other, he refers to transcendental beauty as the harmony of the transcendentals (especially intelligibility, truth, and goodness), taken together.[12] In addition, he also associates beauty with the role of the artists and artistically differentiated consciousness (256). But contemporary art has long made beauty an optional aesthetic principle, so Lonergan's association of beauty with art would need to be nuanced and developed for it to be relevant today.[13]

Intersubjectivity. Lonergan also appears to place the ontic value of a person at the first level of experience. More can be said about this in the next chapter, on meaning. But Lonergan has in mind the spontaneous grasp of value or dignity that one encounters when meeting another person – pre-reflectively, pre-thematized. In *Insight*, he refers to it as spontaneous intersubjectivity (*CWL* 3, 237–9). One spontaneously moves to catch a falling person because one's intersubjectivity is conditioned to respond to that value at a pre-reflective level. Since Lonergan's writing, the work of Emmanuel Levinas (1905–95) has come to the fore and focused on pre-reflective, spontaneous responsibility for the other: Levinas derives an ethics from this intersubjective experience. Likewise, René Girard (1923–2015) focused on the opposite dynamic, where one's intersubjectivity can be unconsciously conditioned to react adversely to the other, especially to one who is deemed as a threat or mimetic rival.[14]

The Scale of Values

Feelings respond to objects in an agreeable or disagreeable manner, and they also respond to values. The values can be either agreeable or disagreeable; but insofar as one chooses value, one chooses genuinely, and insofar as one does not choose value, one chooses disvalue. The habitual choice of value leads to self-transcendence and moral development, and the habitual choice for disvalue leads to personal regression and degeneration.

For Lonergan, feelings do not just respond to values, but do so "in accord with some scale of preference" (32). Lonergan is indebted here to the work of Max Scheler and Dietrich von Hildebrand, and likely drew from both to formulate his own ideas.[15] Lonergan lays out the scale in hierarchical steps as: vital, social, cultural, personal, and religious values. He defines them generally as follows.

Vital values are "health and strength, grace and vigor." These values are preferred to "avoiding the work, privations, pains involved in acquiring, maintaining, restoring them" (33). One may consider the challenge of maintaining a healthy diet, routine of exercise, and discipline around sleep as examples of vital values and the challenges of keeping good healthy habits.[16]

Social values pertain to the collective distribution of goods and the maintenance of structures that "condition the vital values of the whole community" (33). In a society, social values are embodied in the structures of law and order, infrastructure, the economy, and the polity, all of which strive to ensure that the vital values of the collective can be met.[17]

The disvalue in a social context would be self-interest. Members of a community who steal, for example, threaten the good of order, disrupting trust in the community and the economics of exchange. The good of order is an extension of practical intelligence insofar as it emerges in order to solve problems of production, distribution, and regulation of particular goods. Adam Smith, of course, suggested that the basic self-interest of each person is at the root of an economy. To the extent that such a proposition might lead to a justification for individuals hoarding vital values, it runs counter to what Lonergan is conceiving here.

I would add that this *good of order*, which is a term Lonergan often uses to describe social values,[18] also needs to negotiate a proper dialectic of community.[19] The good of order should seek a balance between practical intelligence, on one hand, and spontaneous intersubjectivity, on the other. For example, Japan has a wonderfully efficient social infrastructure (barring the potential for massive earthquakes), but its infrastructure cannot console the portion of its population that at times feels alienated by the strict social mores of a formal society.

Cultural values depend upon vital and social values, but they "rank higher." "It is the function of culture to discover, express, validate, criticize, correct, develop, improve such meaning and value." The first two values (vital and social) pertain to "living and operating," but that is not enough for human beings. Lonergan reminds us that "not on bread alone" do we live (33). We also seek meaning and value over and above merely surviving, or the drudgery that earns us a paycheque. Cultural values such as the creative expression of meaning add something to vital and social values over and above practical utility. "The work of art invites one to withdrawal from practical living and to explore the possibilities of fuller living in a richer world" (63).[20]

The arts can form a basis for critique of social values. One major function of a culture is to clarify the identity of a particular group of people, and to incorporate vital and social values into that narrative and identity in order to elevate and motivate the members. For example, the success or failure of a Japanese multinational corporation is also a success or failure for the Japanese. Second, these cultural values are often expressed in the art, decoration, literature, and history of a people. When there is a question within a culture, or a crisis in which vital and social values are at question, cultural values validate the proper negotiation or mediation of those values. When social and vital values are out of sync, such as a democratic leader becoming too autocratic, cultural values prophetically *criticize*, *correct*, *develop*, and *improve* the situation by supervening in order to correct it. Ionesco's play *Rhinoceros* (1959) concerns a pandemic contagion that is turning everyone into rhinos. As ridiculous as it sounds, the play encourages reflection upon the contagion of fascism and nationalism that swept through Europe during the first part of the twentieth century. More generally, art often functions as a source of critique, whether it be the Dada movement in visual art or, more recently, rap music. Turning to an example that engages a non-artistic cultural value, the "Truth and Reconciliation" initiatives in South Africa, Rwanda, and Canada invoke the values of accountability and reconciliation at a cultural level in order to heal breakdowns in social cooperation by promoting social stability and authentic citizenship.[21]

Personal values. "Personal value is the person in his self-transcendence, as loving and being loved, as originator of values in himself and in his milieu, as an inspiration and invitation to others to do likewise" (33). Lonergan does not specify more precisely what different types of personal values exist. The key to personal values is that they are *personal*. They are choices that flow from one's personal preferences, natural inclinations, interests, and circumstances.

We can take a cue from the existentialist philosopher Kierkegaard, whom Lonergan draws from in his earlier formulation of the good in *Topics in Education* (*CWL* 10). Kierkegaard speaks of three themes in his ethical sphere: marriage, friendship, and vocation. Each of these requires decisions in which individuals make themselves.[22] They involve commitments based on personal discernment, and choices that determine one's horizon of choices (originating value). Marriage or partnership speaks to a commitment to a loved one, friendships reflect the common values and choices among two or more friends, and vocation determines not what I will do for a living per se, but what I will contribute to humankind in how I make my living.

Finally, Lonergan places religious values at the top of the scale. These deal with the orientation of all values towards ultimate transcendence and fulfilment – a topic he addresses in chapter 4 of *Method*.

Two post-Lonergan developments of the preferential scale are noteworthy. The first is the foundational hermeneutics of Lonergan's successor, Robert Doran. Doran argues persuasively that Lonergan's levels of intentional consciousness correlate with each of the levels of the preferential scale.[23]

Experience	→	vital values
Understanding	→	social values
Judgment	→	cultural values
Decision	→	personal values
Love (commitment)	→	religious value

I will prescind for now from speaking about the so-called fifth level of love, and will save that discussion for Lonergan's chapter 4, on religion. Suffice it to say that, in hindsight, Doran's correlation of levels of consciousness with values on the preferential scale fits so adroitly that it now seems almost obvious. The precedent for development comes from Lonergan's treatment of the good in *Topics in Education*, where he correlates the structure of the good (particular goods, the good of order, value) with the levels of experience, understanding, and judgment (*CWL* 10, 41). Although *Topics* is an early formulation of his notion of the good, it at least suggests Lonergan's readiness to ground the structure of the good as isomorphic with and correlative to the levels of consciousness.

Second, Joseph Ogbonnaya has argued that Lonergan's preferential scale of values can ground a sustainable theory of development. While many theories of sustainable development focus on the distribution of vital and social values, his presupposition is that the entire scale can address the manifold challenges that a struggling society may be facing. Personal, cultural, and religious values are just as essential for the long-term sustainable functioning of a society as vital and social values.[24]

Apprehending and Doing the Good   53

Emotional development. Feelings are spontaneous, but insofar as they are "reinforced by advertence and approval" or "curtailed by disapproval," will affect the extent that either of these processes becomes habitual. Consequently, formation and development "will modify one's spontaneous scale of preferences" (33). The implication here, although Lonergan does not spell it out, is that the scale of values can become distorted if one value is habitually preferred at the curtailment of another. Feelings develop and are refined insofar as they are cultivated, reinforced, and procured towards recognizing true value, which in turn fosters self-transcendence. Ideally, this occurs in the various social contexts of formation, such as the family, school, and religion.

While many of our feelings are fleeting, as our conscious attention shifts and responds to varying and changing contexts, some feelings can be more persistent. As a corollary to the previous paragraph, just as feelings can be refined and cultivated, they can be unwanted and so "snapped off by repression," only to reside in the unconscious as long as their relegation there persists. By contrast, there are feelings "so deep and strong, especially when deliberately reinforced, that they channel attention, shape one's horizon, direct one's life" (33). Such feelings persist, for example, when two people are in love. In this case, they are conscious of their abiding feelings of deep resonance, and the privileged intimate connection with the other that flows from a "prior state of being in love." Such a state is the basis of a commitment to a relationship with another person. Lonergan's prose deserves repeating:

> A man or woman that falls in love is engaged in loving not only when attending to the beloved but at all times. Besides particular acts of loving, there is the prior state of being in love, and that prior state is, as it were, the fount of all one's actions. So mutual love is the intertwining of two lives. It transforms an "I" and "thou" into a "we" so intimate, so secure, so permanent, that each attends, imagines, thinks, plans, feels, speaks, acts in concern for both. (33–4)

Another term for the abiding feelings of love and mystery that Lonergan suggests but does not develop is *transcendental feelings*.[25] Those feelings not only move us towards transcendence, but propel us into a new horizon of knowing and choosing: "in full consciousness feelings so deep and strong … they channel attention, shape one's horizon, direct one's life" (34). The notion of transcendental feelings, especially with respect to falling in love, with a human being or with God, is especially helpful because (1) it describes how such feelings orient us towards

54   The Wisdom of Order

another, and (2) in both cases, love for another and love for God, the feelings reorient our horizons vertically into a new expansive horizon. I will return to the notion of a vertical act of finality later.

Distorted Affectivity

Just as we can grasp true values in and through feelings, so too feelings can be distorted, blocked (repressed), or aberrant. Lonergan refers to Friedrich Nietzsche and Max Scheler, especially the latter's work on *ressentiment*.[26] Resentment is a "re-feeling" that flows from a "specific clash with someone else's value qualities." "It is a feeling of hostility, anger, indignation that is neither repudiated nor directly expressed" (34). For example, one might consider Nietzsche's falling-out with his own mentor, Wagner, and the animosity he subsequently felt towards the latter. Lonergan astutely observes that resentment is often fueled by a relationship of power. We are prone to resent someone who is physically, intellectually, morally, or spiritually superior to us, or has some kind of power over our lives (34). There is an entry here for an engagement with the work of Michel Foucault in his emphasis on the role of power in relationships, but that would take us beyond the scope of this project. The work of René Girard and his theory of mimetic envy is also pertinent to any discussion of distorted affectivity. Beneath the unexpressed animosity of the resentful one, Lonergan states, lies an inferiority, an awareness of what one "not only lacked but also feels unequal to acquiring" (34). This is an entry point for a discussion of mimetic envy, which is the basis of Girard's entire work. Resentment against those who possess the "value quality" can lead to a distortion of "the whole scale of values" (34). Indeed, Lonergan declares that "an analysis of *ressentiment* can turn out to be a tool of ethical, social, and historical criticism" (34). This kind of criticism is exactly what Girard offers in his comprehensive analysis of envy – and it is envy that leads to resentment. While it lies beyond the scope of this work, Lonergan's notion of *dramatic bias* also involves distorted affectivity.

The solution to distorted affectivity entails taking "full cognizance" of the entire range of one's affectivity, regardless of how unpleasant the feelings might be.[27] "To take cognizance of them makes it possible for one to know oneself, to uncover the inattention, obtuseness, silliness, irresponsibility that gave rise to the feeling one does not want, and to correct the aberrant attitude" (34). First, "to know oneself" harks back to Lonergan's *Insight*, and his discussion of genuine individuals who scrutinize their own motives and reflect upon their actions (*CWL* 3, 499–504). Second, here we find Lonergan listing the opposite of each of the transcendental precepts: be attentive (inattention), be intelligent (obtuseness), be reasonable (silliness), and be responsible (irresponsibility). Not to take cognizance of one's feelings and their source can lead to a self-alienation between the conscious and unconscious, resulting perhaps in neurosis. As we will see, this self-alienation is the occasion for a further development in Lonergan's notion of conversion, a fourth, psychological conversion.[28]

The Notion of Value

Lonergan discusses value as a *notion*. A transcendental notion is something that one's conscious intentionality anticipates, rather than something one knows. "The transcendental notions are the dynamism of conscious intentionality" (35). As a notion, it anticipates what is to be known in the raising of questions. The notion of intelligibility anticipates intelligibility in answers to the question for intelligence, "What is it?"; the notion of truth anticipates the true and being (existence) in answers to the question for reflection, "Is it so?"; and the notion of value anticipates true value (as opposed to apparent value) in answers to the question for deliberation, "Is it valuable?" We may find this question oddly phrased since more commonly we ask ourselves "What should I do?" But this is exactly what Lonergan means. Our values are reflected in our decisions as two sides of a coin. As we proceed from intelligibility to truth and goodness, we progress to "higher levels of consciousness," promoting ourselves "to full consciousness" and directing ourselves to our goals (35). When we deliberate and decide, we constitute or make ourselves in the world.

The transcendental notions are "broader than any category," but they are not abstract. They are concrete in the sense that the questions arising within the human spirit come directly from the world that human beings encounter. The transcendental notions of the intelligible, the true (and being), and value "also provide the criteria that reveal whether the goals are being reached" (35). The good is concrete, not abstract. This means I should always be able to point to something specific when I say something *is* good, be that a hamburger, a work of art, or a heroic deed.

Lonergan's chapter on the good is significant because in it he clearly distinguishes for the first time the fourth level of operations, decision, in his theory of consciousness. It is a distinct set of operations, but one that is united to the previous three levels. The fourth level involves deliberation, evaluation, decision, and action. One knows when one has made the right decision when one's conscience is eased, and vice versa; a discordant conscience indicates that one has not chosen true value. In a word, the fourth level stands to doing as the second and third levels stand to knowing. More will be said on this later.

Judgments of Value

The transcendental notion of the good, embedded in the structure of the human spirit, manifests itself in questions for deliberation ("Is it valuable; what should I do?") with a goal of goodness that is "beyond criticism." The fruits of this goal are realized by our conscience, which is the normative criterion of the transcendental notion of the good, letting us know when we have made the right decision. A decision flows from a judgment of value, and the two are inextricably intertwined, as two sides of a coin, although, as we will see, the decision flows from a judgment of value as an autonomous spiritual procession.[29] More specifically, the decision proceeds from the grasp of true value (or disvalue) in one's feelings and the corresponding yes or no (this course of action is valuable or not valuable) that proceeds from a judgment of value. The technical way of articulating this here is necessary, since it will come into play in Lonergan's Trinitarian theology, specifically his transposition of the psychological analogy into fourth-level operations.

There are two kinds of judgments of value: simple and comparative. Simple judgments affirm or deny that this specific option is "truly good," and comparative judgments affirm or deny that some specific option is better than another option (37). It is worth noting here that the comparative type of judgment opens the door to the possibility of aesthetic judgment, a topic Kant addressed but Lonergan did not, and that therefore remains to be worked out in Lonergan's philosophy.[30]

Judgments of value are objective insofar as they flow from an authentic self-transcending subject; to the extent that they fail in this regard, they flow from inauthenticity – irresponsibility. "To say that an affirmative judgment of value is true is to say what objectively is or would be good or better. To say that an affirmative judgment of value is false is to say what objectively is not or would not be good or better" (37).

Next, Lonergan specifies the difference between judgments of fact and those of value: "Judgments of value differ in content but not in structure from judgments of fact" (37). Lonergan glides perhaps too quickly over the difference between the two types of judgment, as regards content. In a word, the content of a judgment of fact is truth and reality, and the content of a judgment of value is the good. The former declares what is or is not the case, and the latter approves or disapproves of what is or is not the case.

They are similar in structure in their criterion and meaning. Authenticity in a person's inquiring and deliberating is the criterion for true judgments of fact and true judgments of value. Although the criterion for judgments of fact is cognitive, judgments of value head "towards moral self-transcendence," and are always practical and concrete. In terms of meaning, the truth of both types of judgments is, or claims to be, "independent of the subject" (38). "Judgments of fact state or purport to state what is or is not so; judgments of value state or purport to state what is or is not truly good or really better" (38).

Judgments of value go beyond cognitional self-transcendence, but do not reach the fullness of moral self-transcendence, because that is completed by *doing*. Too often, people know the right thing to do but fail to do it. In doing the right thing they carry out an act of full moral self-transcendence. By carrying out the decision in action, individuals constitute themselves "as proximately capable of moral self-transcendence, of benevolence and beneficence, of true loving" (38).

So, we have Lonergan arguing that judgments of value lie between cognitional judgments of fact and the decision or action by which a person constitutes himself or herself. Moreover, between judgments of fact and judgments of value lies the apprehension of value in or through one's feelings, and such apprehensions follow upon the question, "What ought I do?" (38n17).

Deliberation concerns not the feelings unrelated to objects such as "nonintentional states, trends, urges that are related to efficient [source] and final causes [goals]." Nor does genuine deliberation pertain to feelings related to objects as "agreeable or disagreeable, the pleasant or painful, the satisfying or dissatisfying" (39), although, as we will see, we can confuse these feelings with those that grasp true value. What Lonergan is referring to is the feelings that grasp true value such as "the ontic value of a person or the qualitative value of beauty, understanding, of truth, of noble deeds, of virtuous acts, of great achievements" (39). How do we know when we have grasped true value, that we are doing the right thing? If we are honest and faithful to the transcendental precepts, the questions for moral self-transcendence arise naturally, and we know when we have grasped true value when there are no more relevant questions. As Lonergan suggests, we cannot escape our consciences.

Three elements come together in a judgment of value: (1) knowledge of (human) reality, (2) intentional responses to value, and (3) the initial impulse towards moral self-transcendence that the judgment of value manifests. "The judgement of value presupposes knowledge of human life, of human possibilities proximate and remote, of the probable consequences of projected courses of action" (39). There is a tension to be negotiated between knowledge and feeling. If knowledge of reality is lacking, then reliance upon feelings leads to a moral idealism. On the other hand, it is not enough to rely on feelings alone: they have to be "cultivated, enlightened, strengthened, refined, criticized, and pruned of oddities" (39).

But making the right decision is not just about doing the right thing. Through "existential discovery," we come to realize that such decisions also make us into the kinds of people we will be: authentic or inauthentic. It follows that some decisions are more important than others in that they have a more dramatic role in constituting who we will be. We make decisions (judgments of value) in different contexts. Lonergan has three different contexts in mind: (1) growth, (2) deviations or blocks to growth, and (3) vertical liberty. Together, these three contexts correlate loosely with Lonergan's distinction between progress, decline, and redemption, a distinction he made throughout his career.[31]

In terms of the context of growth, one hopes to proceed habitually according to the preferential scale of values and remain open to further insights, opportunities, and achievements. All things being equal, if one lives in accordance with the transcendental precepts, in which case the affectivity, apprehending true value, is almost a single thrust, then one can simply live by Lonergan's alteration of Saint Augustine's famous phrase: "Love God and do what you wish" (40).

However, "continuous growth seems to be rare" (40). Bias can interfere with one's desire to know the true and do the good. The effects can be devastating and pervasive. At the limit, "one may come to hate the truly good and love the really evil." The effects can be collective, and Lonergan's rhetoric is haunting when he concludes: "such is the monster that has stood forth in our day" (41).

Hope for overcoming the blocks in moral self-transcendence is implied in Lonergan's distinction between vertical and horizontal liberty, which he borrows from Joseph de Finance.[32] Horizontal liberty pertains to the exercise of freedom within a "determinate horizon"; that is, within a set pattern of habits and routines of a particular "existential stance." Likely, Lonergan has the patterns of habits in routine in mind when earlier he invokes "practical autonomy" (*CWL* 12, 179). Vertical liberty is the exercise of freedom that "selects the stance and the corresponding horizon." Such exercises can be implicit, as when one makes decisions that lead one towards authenticity or away from authenticity. They can also be explicit: "then one is responding to the transcendental notion of value, by determining what it would be worthwhile for one to make of oneself, and what it would be worthwhile to do for one's fellow [human beings]" (41). Explicit vertical liberty is a self-conscious commitment, not only to do the right thing, but to commit oneself existentially, in such a manner that subsequent choices will flow from a horizon of previous vertical choices. An explicit act of vertical liberty is represented by a choice of vocation. No doubt, dramatic instances of conversion represent reorientations of one's vertical liberty through grace.

Lonergan undoubtedly has in mind here his own Jesuit formation. The *Spiritual Exercises* of Saint Ignatius comprise a kind of laboratory for the exercise of human freedom. The *Exercises* prepare and move the retreatant towards a climactic choice for God following a meditation on the Two Standards.[33] Most likely, Lonergan had such a choice in mind in his earlier Trinitarian psychological analogy, a decision he calls an exercise of existential autonomy, and which he claims is the most fitting analogy for the processions in the Triune God (*CWL* 12, 179).

The impulse towards vertical liberty is guided by a transcendental notion of value, or a natural desire to do the good and through grace. Confirmation that one is proceeding successfully in this regard takes the form of an "easy conscience." Again, this notion reflects Lonergan's Ignatian formation. In the framework of the *Exercises*, when one makes a discernment (an exercise of existential autonomy), the presence of consolation or desolation serves as an indicator of the correctness of one's decision. Specifically, consolation indicates that one has discerned the proper course of action, and desolation indicates that one may need to rethink one's decision. Of course, one can always fool oneself, and experience what Saint Ignatius calls "false consolation."[34]

Some Clarifications Regarding Lonergan's Fourth-Level Operations[35]

The development of the judgment of value with its integration of feelings in Lonergan's thought was a second milestone in Lonergan's philosophy, according to Robert Doran.[36] It completed the differentiation of the fourth-level operations, decision, and with it, the correlative transcendental precept, *Be responsible*. But Lonergan's treatment of ethics in *Insight* is very different from his treatment of it in *Method*. Although he had not yet fully differentiated decision from judgment at this point in *Insight*, the main difference between the earlier and later accounts of ethics pertains to his engagement with affectivity and its role in judgments of value. In a word, the earlier account, in *Insight*, takes no account of feelings and affectivity in moral deliberation. Moreover, Lonergan does not work out the technicalities of the fourth-level operations in *Insight*, as he does for the second and third levels. Therefore, it is apropos to identify some of those developments. One will be mentioned in connection with Vertin's suggestion of a deliberative insight, which I will return to later in my own proposal to further clarify the fourth-level operations. However, something should be said first of key developments by Doran and Crowe.

Some scholars might be tempted to think that Lonergan's ethics in chapter 18 of *Insight* is no longer necessary. They may view it as an inadequate attempt, conceived prior to his engagement with affectivity. They may not see the value of retaining this earlier work in *Insight*. By contrast, Doran has argued convincingly that the chapter on ethics in *Insight* and the chapter on the human good in *Method* should both be read with the broader context of Lonergan's Ignatian formation in mind. It is not necessary to jettison the ethics of *Insight*; but it is well to situate it in a context that Lonergan was quite familiar with: his own Ignatian formation as a Jesuit.[37]

The emphasis on the "notion of value" in *Insight*, as exemplified in chapter 18, "The Possibility of Ethics," is one where decision and choice flow from an intellectual obligation in rational consciousness: "willing is rational and so moral ... the same intelligent and rational consciousness grounds the doing as well as the knowing [through] the exigence for self-consistency in knowing and doing" (*CWL* 3, 622). There is no explicit or elaborate account of the affectivity in evaluation and decision-making. In such cases, one is impelled by a rational necessity for consistency in one's knowing and doing: "acceding to that demand and deciding reasonably" (*CWL* 3, 637). Those familiar with Lonergan's philosophy will note here that "deciding reasonably" is distinct from his later nomenclature of "deciding responsibly," which he fully differentiates in the first chapter of *Method*. He states on the same page that "the emergence of an obligation is the emergence of rational necessity in rational consciousness" (*CWL* 3, 637). By contrast, in this chapter of *Method*, Lonergan presents the grasp of value in a true judgment of value exclusively as an affective grasp. This development in his thinking may be due to his engagement with phenomenology and existentialism in the invited lectures he gave at Boston College in 1957.[38] He might also have been influenced by his study of feelings and affectivity in connection with his reading of Max Scheler, Dietrich von Hildebrand, and, to some extent, Susanne Langer. These thinkers enabled Lonergan in *Method* to more fully differentiate the fourth level of operations in terms of the subject's affectivity and this latter's role in deliberation, which is implicit in *Insight* but not explicitly differentiated.

In the Ignatian *Spiritual Exercises*, there are three ways in which major decisions or *elections* can occur. In the first moment of election, one can grasp true value immediately and have a clear sense of direction and consolation in one's choice: the will is attracted to the good immediately and "without doubting."[39] In the second moment, which is often more common, one's feelings with respect to a discernment are confused or ambivalent. Adverting to one's affectivity, one discerns true value based on the experiences of consolation and desolation.[40] This is because feelings respond both to satisfactions and to value; therefore, in the *Exercises*, through prayer and spiritual direction, one aims to discern the true value by adverting to and distinguishing the truly valuable over the apparent value or satisfaction. Ignatius proposes rules for discernment that assist one to navigate the maze of one's emotions and authentically tease out the true value over the apparent value, making one's choice clearer.

The third time of election occurs when the affectivity does not pull strongly either way in the discernment. In "a quiet time ... the soul ... uses its natural powers freely and tranquilly."[41] In this case, one invokes the use of one's rationality simply to weigh pros and cons and decide according to the greater-weighted option. In general, if one chooses in accordance with God's will, consolation will follow; if not, desolation will follow.

With provocative and fitting hermeneutics, Doran has pointed out that the ethics of chapter 18 of *Insight* is analogous to the Ignatian third time of election, where the value is not grasped directly by the affectivity (as in the first two times of election), but rather with one's rationality, so that to know the good is to do the good.[42] Let us explain what he means.

In his systematics of the Trinity (*CWL* 12), Lonergan distinguishes three different applications of fourth-level operations as exercises of existential autonomy: practical, speculative-contemplative, and existential (*CWL* 12, 177, 179). Interestingly, most of chapter 18 of *Insight*, a chapter on ethics (fourth level), pertains to the practical. In that chapter, there is mention of the speculative (but mainly in relation to the second level rather than subsequent levels), but nothing explicit on the existential per se, although the existential dimension is hardly absent, given his discussion of moral impotence.[43]

The affective grasp of value is also lacking in Lonergan's fourth-level operations at this stage.[44]

> In *Insight* the good was the intelligent and reasonable. In *Method* the good is a distinct notion. It is intended in questions for deliberation: Is this worthwhile? Is it truly or only apparently good? It is aspired to in the intentional response of feeling to values. It is known in judgments of value made by a virtuous or authentic person with a good conscience. It is brought about

by deciding and living up to one's decisions. Just as intelligence sublates sense, just as reasonableness sublates intelligence, so deliberation sublates and thereby unifies knowing and feeling. (*CWL* 13, 233)

Note that Lonergan delineates the difference between the earlier and later treatments of the good, but he does not negate the earlier version of value. The grasp of value in chapter 18 of *Insight*, I would contend, along with Robert Doran (although he does not use my nomenclature), is a *rational, indirectly affective grasp of value*. By this I mean that, in a rational, indirectly affective grasp of value, as Lonergan envisages it in *Insight*, when deliberating, the judgment of value follows automatically from the judgment of fact as impelled by rational necessity.

Such grasps of true value occur in what Ignatius describes as the third time of election. It does not mean that feelings are not involved in deliberation; therefore, it does not negate Lonergan's comments in *Method* that "apprehensions of value are given in feelings" (37). However, in such times of election, though they be rare, the *direct* apprehension is non-affective and not directly grasped by one's feelings, but through an intellectual grasp of value, although feelings are involved in the deliberation.[45]

These hermeneutics of Doran's that situate Lonergan's early notion of the good as analogous to a third time of election not only are fitting, but also enable us to retain insights from Lonergan's earlier notion, while nonetheless proceeding to his fuller notion of the good in *Method*. But this is not to say that Lonergan's development of fourth-level operations is complete. Frederick Crowe has suggested another important development.

Crowe's Development of Contemplation[46]

Another important development of the deliberation of value was proposed by Frederick E. Crowe. In many of our fourth-level operations we do not just *do*: we can choose to rest in another person, or a beautiful landscape, or contemplate the stars. What Lonergan calls the fourth level, we normally associate with constitutive decision and action. However, Crowe adverts to Aquinas on this point in an attempt to flesh out the latter's notion of will in its active and passive dimensions. Traditionally, the role of the passive will in Lonergan's thought was not emphasized, in part because it is not fully explicated in Aquinas's thought, and Lonergan relied on Aquinas. Crowe seeks to flesh out the passive and active dimensions of fourth-level operations as *complacency* and *concern*, respectively.[47] He admits that *complacency* is not an ideal term, given its connotation with inertness in English; nevertheless, he settles on the term. Crowe's lengthy exegesis of the relevant passages in Aquinas need not be summarized here; what interests us in these pages is that Crowe argues for two ways in which the fourth-level operations function: the *via receptionis* and the *via motionis*.[48] The former pertains to the will as an end to the rational act, and the latter refers to the will as the principle. Crowe spends the bulk of his essay arguing for the *via receptionis*, but this by way of contrast with the *via motionis*, since it is neglected in Aquinas's thought. Crowe's Thomistic hermeneutics seeks to bring back the emphasis on the *via receptionis*, or passive aspect of the will. He does this with "the conviction that it is the Cinderella of studies in psychology and spirituality, chronically pushed off the stage by the more palpably evident activity of the will in active pursuit of the good."[49] Certainly the existentialists assisted in "pushing aside" the passive or receptive aspect of deliberative cognitional operations in their emphasis on self-constitution. Even Lonergan himself seems to bypass its importance. Hence, as Lonergan scholars who seek to clarify and fill out his fourth-level operations, we will need to account for its receptive, contemplative dimension.

Fourth-Level Operations: Insights?

The question emerges whether the grasp of value in feelings and the judgment of value that follows function like insights in the sense of the simple and reflective insights of the second and third levels respectively, or are they actually insights but in a different order? When Michael Vertin posited a deliberative insight, he was presuming insights to exist at the fourth level, although the content of such an insight would be true value, as opposed to the content of the second level, which is (potential) intelligibility, and the genuine content of the third level, which is truth-existence.[50] We have seen that the content is different because judgments of fact pertain to truth and reality, and judgments of value pertain to the good (although subsuming judgments of fact). Vertin believes that the structure of judgments of value is analogous to the third level (judgments of fact).[51] In turn, he argues for a deliberative insight, an insight that tells the subject that he or she can make a decision. By contrast, Doran views the two steps in the fourth level as analogous to the second and third levels combined. Those two steps would be (1) the judgment of value and (2) the decision (*TDH*, 57–8).

I believe Doran's take on the structure is more fitting because it coheres with a possible grasp of value at the fourth level, just as the second level's grasp of intelligibility is potentially true. The fittingness also pertains to the context of the three times of election discussed earlier. However, if the structures of judgments of fact and judgments of value are similar, then would not there have to be something analogous to the reflective insight of a judgment of fact in the judgment of value? Here, Vertin's notion of a deliberative insight can contribute to fleshing out the structure in a judgment of value especially as the true judgment of value issues fourth a decision.

I would explicate the similar structures between the two types of judgment further by positing an *evaluative insight* that grasps (possible) value, much like how basic insight at the second level grasps the potentially true. Then, borrowing Vertin's nomenclature, there is a *deliberative insight*, a grasp of true value. The deliberative insight functions in a similar manner to a reflective insight, but at the fourth level. It assures me that I have made the right choice, that I have grasped true value, whereas the reflective insight assures me that my judgment of fact is true because it indicates that all the conditions for a specific query have been fulfilled. Similarly, the evaluative insight grasps possible courses of action, while the deliberative insight settles on the correct course of action, based on the process of discernment.

Beliefs

In the next section, Lonergan turns to a discussion of beliefs and their relation to a judgment of value. On one hand, this section might appear to be out of place; on the other, it needs to be seen in the context of his earlier work on belief in *Insight* – the difference between a judgment of fact *as immanently generated knowledge* and a judgment of fact from another *believed* as a necessary part of the cumulation of human knowledge. The belief Lonergan has in mind here is not religious belief per se, for that is more specifically addressed in chapter 4, on religion. Still, the fact that he addresses it in chapter 20 of *Insight*, a chapter dedicated to special transcendent knowledge (i.e., grace), suggests that, in his mind, the topic was occasioned by the contents of that chapter: otherwise, one would have expected him to treat it earlier in *Insight*, perhaps in chapters 9 and 10, on judgment, or chapter 18, on ethics.

Keep in mind that we memorize our multiplication tables in elementary school and do not question their veracity because we presume that they rest on previously acquired knowledge. It is a knowledge acquired by others, who have worked out the original calculations, and so such knowledge reflects their true judgments that are virtually unconditioned. This prevents us from tediously working out all the previous calculations on our own. "The typical process of belief is from knowledge in one mind to belief in the same truth in another mind" (*CWL* 3, 739). Just as we believe the judgments of facts of others, so, too, we accept as good those things that other people have affirmed to be truly good. In so doing, we can avoid some painful mistakes in our own striving for the good. In *Method*, Lonergan is expanding his notion of belief from judgments of fact to judgments of value, or, at the very least, he is making it explicit in the fourth level.

Let's review what he says about belief in *Insight*. "The general context of belief is the collaboration of [hu]mankind in the advancement and the dissemination of knowledge" (*CWL* 3 725). To that common fund, researchers can contribute their own "immanently generated insights" – in a word, their own unique discoveries. But most of our knowledge is received from others as "reliably communicated knowledge," the rationally affirmed insights of others. The reception of that knowledge from others is called *belief*. "There are extraordinarily few items of immanently generated knowledge that are totally independent of beliefs … and in that process personal knowledge and belief practice an unrelenting symbiosis" (*CWL* 3, 728). Lonergan suggests that the web of immanently generated knowledge and belief in the habitual memory of our minds also needs to be appropriated, and so that appropriation is immanent insofar as I make it my own: "every belief and all its implications have been submitted to the endlessly repeated, if unnoticed, test of fresh experiences, of further questions and new insights, of clarifying and qualifying revisions of judgment" (*CWL* 3, 728).

Lonergan incorporates the fourth level of operations in its nascent development in *Insight*, where he calls it *rational self-consciousness*, as distinct from *rational consciousness*, which refers to the third level, *judgment*. "The general context of belief, then, is a sustained collaboration of many instances of rational self-consciousness in the attainment and the dissemination of knowledge" (*CWL* 3, 728). As we will see, belief as knowledge requires an assent of one's rational self-consciousness – a decision to believe.

The logical possibility of belief rests on a theorem that involves two parts: (1) a remote and general part, and (2) a proximate and concrete part. With respect to the first, the attainment of truth rests on the subject's grasp of a virtually unconditioned. That grasp means that the truth obtained is independent of the subject and the time and place in which the grasp occurs. Just as the grasp is attainable, so too it must be communicable to another time or place. With respect to the second, the proximate and concrete pertains to judgments of fact. There arises a common fund of shared knowledge that contains the judgments of facts of others. To that fund, one must make one's own intelligent and critical appropriations, insofar as one believes them to be true (*CWL* 3, 728).

Lonergan proceeds to outline the five aspects of belief; but his context is that of believing others' judgments of fact. He outlines the five steps to belief in *Insight* as being:

(1) preliminary judgments on the value of belief in general, on the reliability of the source for this belief, and on the accuracy of the communication from the source,
(2) a reflective act of understanding that, in virtue of the preliminary judgments, grasps as virtually unconditioned the value of deciding to believe some particular proposition,
(3) the consequent judgment of value,
(4) the consequent decision of the will, and
(5) the assent that is the act of believing. (*CWL* 3, 729–30) 4

Lonergan expands in the same work on each of these five steps to belief, addressing the first, last. Here I begin with that one.

1. *Preliminary judgments on the value of belief in general, on the reliability of the source for this belief, and on the accuracy of the communication from the source*

   There are no prefabricated general rules to discern in advance judgments of fact. It is not always feasible to take people at their word or sources at face value; reliability and accuracy need to be scrutinized. There may be different procedures for scrutinizing, but, to the extent that there is a general rule, it lies in Lonergan's basic philosophical position: "to be alertly intelligent and critically reflective; and however intelligent and critical one may be, the result to be named not knowledge but belief, one ends with an assent to a proposition that one could not oneself grasp to be unconditioned" (*CWL* 3, 733).

   Moreover, Lonergan states that "the scrutiny of the reasons for almost any belief will reveal that it rests on other beliefs" (*CWL* 3, 733). The point is that, while much of our knowledge relies on belief (the affirmed judgments of others), this is not a reason for scepticism, for that would only bring about intellectual paralysis. Lonergan is confident that if one examines one's own conscious interiority properly, one will discover the ability to make true judgments, to grasp the virtually unconditioned: "belief is possible because the criterion of truth is the unconditioned" (*CWL* 3, 233). The affirmation of this process in oneself, given the immanent critical role of the intellect, establishes a reasonable basis for taking the judgments of others as knowledge.

2. *A reflective act of understanding that, in virtue of the preliminary judgments, grasps as virtually unconditioned the value of deciding to believe some particular proposition*

For Lonergan, this second is the "key act." It is the goal that the preliminary judgments anticipate, and it is the basis from which the subsequent three acts flow. The reflective act occurs insofar as the conditions have been fulfilled in the preliminary judgments in order to affirm the value of believing the person, source, or text. In other words, there are no other relevant questions as to whether the person, source, or text should or should not be believed. The conditions, as fulfilled, grasp the virtually unconditioned so that the person, place, or text should be believed.

3. *The consequent judgment of value*

The judgment of value "of deciding to believe … proceeds with rational necessity from one's own grasp of the virtually unconditioned." As a value judgment, it differs from judgments of fact because it concerns "the good of the intellect" with respect to a "a particular belief." It is different from other judgments of value because it declares the value of "accepting from others in a determinate instance what they communicate as unconditioned" (CWL 3 730).

4. *The consequent decision of the will*

The decision is a "free and responsible decision of the will to believe a given proposition as probably or certainly true or false." First, it is a "reasonable act of the will" if it flows from a "favorable judgment on the value of deciding to believe the proposition in question." Second, it is a "good act of the will" insofar as "the favorable judgment of value also is correct" (CWL 3, 730). Third, in its "antecedents," the decision to believe is similar to other decisions, insofar as "it presupposes the occurrence of rational reflection in which one grasps believing as a possible course of action, and, further, it presupposes the occurrence of rational reflection in which the course of action is evaluated favorably." Fourth, the decision to believe flows from the judgment of value. It differs in its consequences relative to other kinds of decisions, such as physical actions, changing the focus of one's attention, or existential acts of autonomy. Rather, the decision to believe is "a decision to produce in intellect the act of assenting to a proposition or dissenting from it" (CWL 3, 731).

5. *The assent that is the act of believing*

The act of believing is an "act of rational self-consciousness" in the context of collaboration towards the advancement of knowledge. It resembles other such judgments in "object and in mode," but it differs in "motive and in origin." With respect to object, it declares that a proposition is true or false. With respect to mode, it answers yes or no with certainty or probability. The difference in motive is that one accepts or rejects a belief "motivated by a decision to profit by a human collaboration in the pursuit of truth." In terms of origin, rather than the origin being in "a reflective grasp of the unconditioned" immanently within an autonomous subject, the origin lies in some other person's grasp of the unconditioned (CWL 3, 731).

Lonergan's treatment of knowledge as belief in *Insight* is nuanced and sophisticated. Of course, beliefs can be mistaken, since other people's knowledge can be mistaken; but we also have the critical intelligence to scrutinize those mistakes. Lonergan addresses this in the same section on belief in *Insight*, but the issues can also be addressed in the chapter on dialectic, since much of human education involves "demythologization."

Belief in Method

In *Method*, Lonergan identifies the steps to belief a little differently than in *Insight*. They are as follows:

(1) A report by someone who affirms or denies
(2) The general judgment of value
(3) A particular judgment of value
(4) The decision to believe
(5) The act of believing (45–7)

Lonergan suggests that in his treatment of belief in *Method*, there is something new vis-à-vis his treatment of it in *Insight* (42n26). Here we see Lonergan transposing what he said earlier about belief in *Insight* into *Method* in terms of *value*. To be sure, belief in *Insight* is a judgment of value, but the value in question was the value of believing, while the particular object of that belief was knowledge as discovered or communicated through someone else. In *Insight*, he is demonstrating how our judgments of fact are passed on into communal knowledge of belief. Lonergan is also presuming the convertibility of the transcendentals of the true and the good. This means that a correct judgment of value is true. In a word, we believe other people's true judgments of fact (1) because they are true (resulting from a grasp of the virtually unconditioned), and (2) out of the practical necessity of not starting from scratch in our basic inquiries, which would involve what Lonergan calls a "return to primitivism" (44).

In *Method*, Lonergan is showing how this process of belief applies also explicitly to judgments of value. First, an act of believing includes the fourth-level operations (decision-action). This is implied in his discussion of knowledge as belief in *Insight*, as is evident in points 3–5 of the list of steps from *Insight*. Second, as our knowledge is believed, so what we value is passed on as well. The Ten Commandments, for example, are the collective wisdom of a historical community to manage conflict in society. We can learn by others' mistakes by assenting to the values they come to assent to, often hard won in social conflicts. It goes without saying that assenting to common values for the greater good is a perennial challenge for human existence. Moreover, belief is possible "because what is true is of itself not private but public, not something confined to the mind that grasps it, but something independent of that mind and so in a sense detachable and communicable" (45).

In some ways, Lonergan's treatment in *Method* is more succinct and straightforward. Whereas in *Insight* the first step is "preliminary judgments on the value of belief in general, on the reliability of the source for this belief, and on the accuracy of the communication from the source," in *Method* "the preliminary judgment on the value of belief in general" is now the second step. Moreover, the second of the three preliminary judgments that comprise step 1 from *Insight* ("the reliability of the source for this belief" and the "accuracy of the communication from the source") Lonergan has relegated in *Method* to the third step, as a particular value of judgment. This is to say, he is presuming that, before one assents or declines to believe, one has scrutinized the source for credibility. This also suggests that the judgment of value itself has conditions that need to be met just as does the judgment of fact (45).

Lonergan's conception of knowledge and decision as belief does not detract from our ability to have immanently generated knowledge (to discover our own truths) or immanently generated benevolence; but it is humbling to consider how much of our knowledge comes to us via belief, rests on the true judgments of facts of others. To scrutinize beliefs may be called for, but a critical appropriation of certain beliefs does not discredit the notion of belief. Nor does knowledge as belief open knowledge up to the charge of subjectivism, for true knowledge rests on a grasp of the virtually unconditioned. To eschew belief as knowledge is to bring about a paralysis and to burden ourselves with the impossible task of getting even menial tasks completed without being able to rely on beliefs learned from others.

The Structure of the Human Good

"The human good, then, is at once individual and social" (51). In the next section of *Method*, Lonergan outlines the structure of the good and how exactly the individual good is related to the social or communal good. He presents the following schema (*CWL* 14, 47):

	Individual		
Potentiality	Actuation	Social	Ends
capacity, need	operation	cooperation	particular good
plasticity, perfectability	development, skill	institution, role, task	good of order
liberty	orientation, conversion	personal relations	terminal value

He then proceeds to elaborate on the schema, but not in the linear left-to-right order one would expect. First, he begins with the individuals who have the capacity (ability) to operate (build, construct, make, create) particular goods (food, shelter, etc.) to meet needs or wants (health, safety, luxury items) at any one time or place.

Second, he relates the individual to the social. The way individuals make a living is through *cooperating* in the larger economic context. This also requires *institutions* (family, social mores, society, education, law, economy, technology, and faith groups). These institutions determine the fixed pattern of *roles* and *tasks*, although these roles are open to generational changes, which can be slow.

Third, the individual is further related to a contribution to the good of order. Individuals have the capacity to develop and hone skills in order to meet the roles and tasks of the institution. They do so towards particular ends, to be sure, but they also do so within the larger good of order. The good of order is concrete: for example, traffic signals are part of that order, but presume the cooperation of those operating vehicles. This good of order is concrete and concerns the recurrent, sustained, and interdependent distribution of particular goods.

Fourth, Lonergan relates all of the terms in the third row. Liberty is the individual's ability to self-determine his or her attitudes and actions. We can choose from various courses of actions. As oriented towards moral self-transcendence, we can freely choose true value. Insofar as this occurs, we become creators or origins of terminal value, or originating value. We participate in the good of order, thus facilitating particular goods. However, we can also be disoriented away from transcendence and limit our decisions with selfish motives, or simply to avoid pain and pursue pleasure. To do so is to fail in authenticity and service to the greater good.

"Terminal values are the values that are chosen; true instances of the particular good, a true good of order, a true scale of preferences regarding values and satisfactions" (50). Individuals' basic goodness, that is to say, their orientation within a community, is a native orientation towards the transcendental notions of understanding, truth, and goodness. However, it is an orientation that requires commitment, development, and refinement. When there are lapses or blocks in the latter, conversion heals those blocks and reorients one towards understanding, truth, goodness, and love.

Lonergan summarizes the structure of the human good:

> The human good, then, is at once individual and social. Individuals do not just operate to meet their needs but cooperate to meet one another's needs. As the community develops its institutions to facilitate cooperation, so individuals develop skills to fulfill the roles and perform the tasks set by the institutional framework. Though the roles are fulfilled and the tasks are performed that the needs be met, still all is done not blindly but knowingly, not necessarily but freely. The process is not merely the service of [humanity]; it is above all the making of [humanity, its] advance in authenticity, the fulfilment of [one's] affectivity, and the direction of [one's] work to the particular goods and a good of order that are worthwhile. (51)

But Lonergan is not naive. He is aware of how sin and bias can erode and destroy the structure. He acknowledges this in the final section of the chapter, "Progress and Decline."

Progress and Decline

"As self-transcendence promotes progress, so the refusal of self-transcendence turns progress into cumulative decline" (54). The implications of what Lonergan is saying in this section are cogent and relevant for any age, but especially following the century in which he is writing.

In this section, Lonergan speaks about how a collective of individuals or a community possesses a basic orientation towards self-transcendence and development, but also a simultaneous orientation towards decline and destruction.

Lonergan mentions three biases that pertain to the individual and the collective alike. Egoistic bias is the bias of selfishness, where one chooses what is best for oneself at the expense of the greater good. Group bias pertains to the rivalry and conflict between groups, which can be motivated even by outright hatred. General bias praises practical knowledge and eschews theoretical knowledge; in short, it restricts questions that might lead to longer-term solutions, and is satisfied with short-term solutions and their implications. The collective effects of these three biases on a society in their milder or corrosive forms lead to widespread moral compromise, corruption, and injustice; at the limit, they lead to its destruction.

Anyone with a rudimentary understanding of Lonergan's thought on bias, especially in *Insight*, might wonder why he is not including dramatic bias in the discussion on decline. First, as laid out in chapter 6 of *Insight*, dramatic bias is not associated with moral culpability, as are the other three biases. Second, it may be that Lonergan did not develop dramatic bias much beyond the psychoanalytic theorists with whom he engaged. Subsequent developments in psychology, post-traumatic stress, and the theories of Girard on the role of unconscious processes that lead to violence reveal how dramatic bias can act as a propellant for the other three biases. According to Girard, we can learn to hate the rival. Something like this is implied, for example, in Lonergan's discussion of group biases, when he declares: "Hostile groups do not easily forget their grievances, drop their resentments, overcome their fears and suspicions" (52). In this way, dramatic bias interpenetrates with group bias.

Lonergan reiterates that what makes one "properly" oriented to understanding, truth, and goodness is the extent to which one adheres to the transcendental precepts; that is, to the extent that one is attentive to one's experience, intelligent in one's understanding, reasonable in one's judgments, and responsible in one's decisions. To do this is to be true to oneself – it is to encounter one's true self. Conversely, not to adhere to the transcendental precepts, to go against them, is what Lonergan defines as alienation. One is alienated from oneself to the extent that one ignores the transcendental precepts. The cumulative effects of decline, that is, of "inattention, obtuseness, unreasonableness, irresponsibility," lead to increasing corruption, the perpetuation of ideologies, and violence. Human efforts alone cannot curb increasing violence. His diagnosis and prognosis are ever relevant:

Corrupt minds have a flair for picking the mistaken solution and insisting that it alone is intelligent, reasonable, good. Imperceptibly the corruption spreads from the harsh sphere of material advantage and power to the mass media, the stylish journals, the literary movements, the educational process, the reigning philosophies. A civilization in decline digs its own grave with a relentless consistency. It cannot be argued out of its destructive ways. (53–4)

Still, Lonergan does not leave us without hope. Besides progress (via the transcendental precepts) and decline (resulting from bias), there is the hope of redemption (God's self-communication through grace). This particularly pertains to self-sacrificing love, which Lonergan takes up in more detail in the chapter on religion. Genuine religion promotes justice, but it also promotes self-sacrificing love – therein lies the hope for redemption and the reversal of decline (54).

Before that chapter, however, Lonergan outlines the different ways in which consciousness can flow and meaning can be expressed. This enables him to put forth a philosophical understanding of pluralism in the chapter on meaning, to which we turn next.

4 Different Types of Meaning

The study of meaning is an important precursor for addressing method. If one grasps the different kinds of meaning encountered in human living, one will be prepared to understand the different kinds of expressions addressed in the functional specialties interpretation, history, systematics, and communications. It will also help to understand the different manners in which religious experience is expressed. In this chapter, Lonergan reviews the types, elements, functions, realms, and stages of meaning.

Types of Meaning

Intersubjectivity and Intersubjective Meaning

There is a spontaneous intersubjectivity that functions as if there is a "prior we" before we experience ourselves as individuals. It is *functional* in that we automatically reach out to catch a falling person, and it is *vital* in that it is instinctual – we are compelled. That said, one might consider it possible for a society to have eroded its spontaneous intersubjectivity, and this is perhaps a society to be avoided – one where civility and decency are wanting.

Lonergan again draws on the work of Max Scheler, who distinguishes community of feeling, fellow-feeling, psychic contagion, and emotional identification. The first two are intentional responses to situations, and the second two are vital (instinctual responses). In community of feeling, two or more people simultaneously respond in kind to the same object, such as an emotional movie. In fellow-feeling, one person's emotional response to an object evokes an emotional response from another person; but the second person is responding to the first person's emotions, not to the cause (object) of the emotions per se. In a word, we can be moved by another person as the emotions of another function as the intentional object for our affective response.

"Psychic contagion is a matter of sharing another's emotion without adverting to the object of the emotion" (56). This occurs when one becomes spontaneously caught up in the emotions of a crowd. In our digital age, this can occur when a video goes viral, provoking an overwhelming collective response. The primal nature of such emotions can be exploited by leaders or others with their own ideological agendas.

Emotional identification is withdrawing from one's own personal differentiation and identifying with another human being as a "vital unity." This can occur in the context of the maternal love for a newborn, the play of a child with a doll, sexual intercourse, support for a team in sports, and the like.

Intersubjective Meaning

Human intersubjectivity has its own kind of "embodiment of meaning" (59). Prior to the spoken word, human beings can communicate intersubjectively non-verbally. Lonergan exposits on the phenomenology of a smile and its universal significance. It is perceptible, natural, and spontaneous, a gestalt with a patterned set of variable movements. We discover the meaning of a smile through our encounters with others: it is not taught in words. We also learn from context that it can have different meanings: joy, mendaciousness, and so on. Lonergan contrasts the smile with linguistic meaning in the following way (59):

Linguistic	Smile
Univocal	Multivocal (different) meanings
True in two ways	True in one way
Contains distinctions (propositions)	Concrete (global) meaning (fact)
Objective (meaning objectified)	Intersubjective

In general, linguistic meaning is univocal (excluding creative writing); that is, it has one meaning. In contrast, smiles can have different meanings, depending on the context and the intention of the one smiling.

Linguistic meaning can be true in terms of a proposition, or true with respect to reality. Linguistic meanings contain distinctions and can be expressed in propositions. The meaning of a smile is universal and immediate; it is a fact, rather than a proposition. Finally, linguistic meaning objectifies or embodies meaning in language, while a smile or non-verbal meaning is intersubjective; it reveals one subject to another in a spontaneous, immediate manner.

Art. Lonergan gleans a definition of art from Susanne Langer; he defines art as "the objectification of the purely experiential pattern" (60).[1] He breaks down the definition. Patterns can be abstract, as in the case of the musical arts, or concrete, as in the case of the visual arts. Next, "the pattern of perceiving is an experiential pattern" (60). The pattern stands out precisely as a pattern rather than as cacophony. He suggests that the perceptibility of patterns (especially aesthetic patterns) readily stands out because they draw upon "organic analogies." In this, Lonergan concurs with the architect Christopher Alexander, who argues that beautiful architecture mimics natural beauty.[2]

The pattern is pure because it is not instrumentalized by the practical affairs of everyday living (an instrumentalization heightened by the rise of the digital age and preoccupation with hand-held digital devices), the intellectual or scientific world of concepts, or theories, or conditioned by an "a priori theory of experience" that leads to a divided epistemology that views "impressions as objective" and "patterns as subjective." Utilitarianism would attend to objects only "in the measure there is something in them for me to get out of them" (60).

The purely experiential pattern is enriching rather than impoverishing, and it finds "its full complement in feeling" (61). There is a natural unfolding pattern that would see the experiences as sequences of precious moments linked together like pearls in a necklace – one precious moment after another.

Meaning as experienced, understood, and judged pertains to what is meant. "But the experiential pattern is elemental" (61). Elemental meaning pertains to the non-instrumentalized consciousness momentarily free, as long as it lasts, from practical affairs and temporal obligations. With elemental meaning, one "has ceased to be a responsible inquirer" and has rather come to enjoy "emergent, ecstatic, originating freedom" (61). Art criticism and history can comment on the works of art, and perhaps informatively so; but they cannot recapture the experience of elemental meaning.

The goal of the artist is to express this elemental meaning in a certain artistic medium. The creative act involves an insight into the purely experiential pattern that the artist seeks to express. But even the artist does so with a "psychic distance" that enables her to recollect the "emotion in tranquility." For example, the artist reflects on "terror" not from a place of elemental terror, but from a space of tranquillity that enables her to express the image of terror in her artwork. She does it in such a way that provokes the observer to pass over to the experience as mediated through the work. The observer participates in the artwork, thus getting a momentary reprieve from everyday affairs, and receiving an expanded, fuller sense of living.

One significance of this view of art is that it emphasizes the unique intelligence of artists and their role in enriching our world.[3]

Symbols. "A symbol is an image of a real or imaginary object that evokes a feeling or is evoked by a feeling" (62). Symbols can be related to objects, other feelings, or a subject. Different symbols have different effects on different people, depending on development, contexts, and other factors. However, there can be blocks in affective development, distortions of which can be drawn out by symbols. Symbols can also contain opposing meanings: for example, the symbols in the legend of Saint George and the Dragon contain the dramatic elements of two opposing forces. The healing of blocks in affective development will involve a "transvaluation and transformation of symbols." A symbol that once frightened, no longer does (64).

Symbols differ from logic in that symbols can express contradictory feelings while logic cannot. The coinciding of opposites is often depicted in symbols of art. In this way, symbols can express internal existential dilemmas and tensions in ways that logic is unable to do. Moreover, symbols complement logic in that they meet the "need for internal communication": the body, mind, and affectivity communicate with each other through symbols (64–5).

It is worth noting that Robert Doran's notion of psychic conversion, as it pertains to the healing of a block in internal communication, is apposite here. Doran has in mind the communication of the body with the mind, where the psychic censor may prevent images that would otherwise lead to insight. The key to healing that repressive censor would be a restoration of internal communication, which would effect the restoration of a flow of images and symbols.[4]

Lonergan traces the study of symbols from its roots in the psychoanalysis of internal communication to more current studies from the twentieth century. The genesis of psychoanalysis with Freud, Adler, and Jung occasioned the modern study of symbols. From there, the study of symbolism made its way into other disciplines, such as literature (Northrop Frye) and religious studies (Mircea Eliade).

Doran raised the question, in connection with Lonergan's analysis, of the extent to which symbols can be explanatory rather than descriptions. Symbols as descriptions relate the world of things to individuals or communities; explanatory symbols relate things to one another. Normally, explanatory knowledge pertains to world theory, while the world of symbol originates in the subject and is expressed in community, which is concrete rather than theoretical. However, prolonged Jungian psychoanalysis begins to view symbols as related to one another, as they manifest themselves in the analysand's dream reports. From here, effective treatment entails bringing the complexes to consciousness so they can be healed. For Doran, this situating of symbols in relation to one another over a period comprises an explanatory function of symbols (*TDH*, 61).

In my own work, I have argued that there is an explanatory function to symbols in a communal context.[5] Rather than relating the symbols to one another, I have argued that the various meanings ascribed to communal symbols of identity, by virtue of the multivalence of such symbols, function in an explanatory way. For Christians, the cross represents many fundamental meanings, and those meanings can be related to one another in an explanatory manner. It is not necessary to discuss the explanatory possibility of symbol further here; I have simply flagged some potential developments of Lonergan's approach. The nature of theological inquiry lends itself to symbolic as well as rational syntheses. Such a notion may be important if Doran is correct that systematic theology must invoke aesthetic-dramatic meaning as well as more abstract technical vocabulary.[6]

Linguistic Meaning

With language, "meaning finds its greatest liberation" (67). Consider that once human beings developed the ability to communicate through signed, spoken, and written language, a whole range of possibilities opened up for human development. One is reminded of Helen Keller's discovery of communication and how it took her out of existential alienation and gave her access to a community.

Lonergan discusses three types of language: common-sense, technical, and literary. Common-sense language confines itself to the world of practical living, getting things done, and the drama of human relations. It reflects the world of things related to the subject. It is "transient" in that it develops and comes and goes based on changing contexts and use. With the division of labour, language develops that is common to those of a specific division. Hence, specialized common-sense or technical language develops as different fields of study and divisions of labour emerge. Literary language is more permanent because it records the timeless creativity of the human spirit, studied by subsequent generations. It "floats somewhere in between logic and symbol" (70). Literary language expresses feeling, and it does so through the language of symbol and metaphor. Its goal is not just to communicate cognitively, but affectively as well.

Incarnate Meaning

Incarnate meaning is the meaning of a person, of one's life, words, and deeds, communicated by means of any of the previous kinds of meaning. It can be applied to individuals or groups, or it can be "transposed" archetypically to characters in performing art. The opposite of incarnate meaning would be meaningless expressions. The fact that Lonergan leads this short section on incarnate meaning with the motto from John Henry Newman's coat-of-arms, *Cor ad cor loquitur*, suggests that incarnate meaning is a person communicating with someone else though an affective connection.

Elements of Meaning

Next, Lonergan turns to the elements of meaning, which he divides in terms of *sources*, *acts*, and *terms of meaning*. The sources are any place in which meaning originates; for Lonergan, the sources are always in the human mind. The sources will be "all conscious acts and all intended contents, whether in the dream state or on any of the four levels of waking consciousness" (71). Further, a source can be either (1) transcendental, originating from "the very dynamism of human consciousness" (that is, this is where questions originate), or (2) categorial, the determinations from each of the four levels of intentional consciousness. Often, the categorial are the answers to the questions arising from the levels (71).

Lonergan introduces further nomenclature to distinguishes the various acts of meaning. He refers to them as potential, formal, full, active, and instrumental acts of meaning. Each act originates in the levels of consciousness so that:

– Potential → acts of sensing and acts of understanding (insight into potential intelligibility in the data or the relations among the data)
– Formal → acts of conceiving, thinking, considering, defining supposing, formulating
– Full → act of judgment (reflective insight)
– Active meanings (constitutive and effective) and instrumental (expressive) acts → decision (action – communication) (72).[7]

Lonergan developed the notion of potential (elemental) meaning sometime in between his original formulation of the structure of meaning and the writing of *Method*. At the level of elemental meaning, there is not yet a "distinction between meaning and meant." (72).

Prima facie, a smile, work of art, or symbol possesses unarticulated or unexpressed meaning. Insofar as it has yet to be expressed, it is said to have potential meaning. Likewise, sensible data and data of consciousness have potential intelligibility; as carriers of potential meaning, they are subject to the scrutiny of judgment or a formal act of meaning that differentiates meaning from meant.

Formal acts of meaning occur at the second level of consciousness, understanding, although the insight or act of understanding, the insight with potential intelligibility, technically occurs at the second level as well. Once formulated, the distinction between meaning and meant occurs but as *an object of thought*. It is the object of the acts of "conceiving, thinking, considering, defining, supposing, formulating" (72). However, at this point, "the precise nature of the distinction" between meaning and meant has yet to fully occur in the process of human knowing. There is meaning but only in thought; the question for the next level, judgment, is whether the meaning occurs in reality. For example, unicorns exist in the imagination, but not in reality, as horses do, so we would say that a unicorn has formal meaning. By contrast: "The full act of meaning is an act of judging. One settles the status of the object of thought, that it is merely an object of thought, or mathematical entity, or a real thing lying in the world of experience or a transcendent reality beyond the world" (72).

When Lonergan speaks of active meanings, he is no longer distinguishing between meaning and meant so much as between meaning and the creation of meaning. Active meanings pertain to fourth-level operations (deliberation, evaluation, decision, and action). An instrumental act of meaning (or communicative act of meaning) pertains to any externalized expression of which human beings are capable. Effective acts of meaning make or do things. Constitutive acts of meaning establish the basic values of a person or community. Lonergan will return to effective and constitutive acts at a future point. There is a subset of instrumental meaning referred to as performative meaning. It "is constitutive or effective meaning linguistically expressed" (72n31). An example would be a person bequeathing something in a will, or a military commander giving an order to subordinates.

"A term of meaning [goal or end point] is what is meant" (73). The term of potential meaning has not yet distinguished between meaning and meant; the term of formal acts of meaning has distinguished meaning from meant, but has not yet settled on the ontological status (an object of thought versus an object in reality). The term of a full act of meaning is certain or probable knowledge of reality. The term of constitutive acts of meaning expresses an individual or community's values and beliefs. The term of effective acts of meaning pertains to the actions that an individual or community has taken.

Next, Lonergan distinguishes three spheres of being that full acts of meaning can determine: real, restricted, and transcendent. Real spheres of being pertain to that which exists. Restricted spheres pertain to the level of intelligence concerned with mathematical and logical reasoning, hypothesizing, and so on. While restricted and real spheres rest on true judgments, the conditions for real spheres are fuller and lie in the data of sense and consciousness. "But the spheres differ so vastly because the conditions to be fulfilled differ" (73). An unverified hypothesis (restricted sphere) may be "true" as a coherent surmise of ordered intelligible relations among data, but it could also be a mistaken view or misinterpretation of the data. Mathematics and logic are limited because their spheres do not necessitate any reference to sensible or conscious data. Finally, the transcendent sphere of being is the ground of reality; unlike the real sphere, which rests on conditions, transcendent being is formally unconditioned – it has no conditions.[8]

Functions of Meaning

In this section, Lonergan shifts the topic to how meaning works in human society. There is some overlap from the previous section because some of the goals and functions of meaning are synonymous. Functions of meaning are cognitive, efficient, constitutive, and communicative. From here, he discusses community, existence, and history, as these topics arise naturally following an investigation of constitutive and communicative functions of meaning.

The cognitive function of meaning pertains to meaning not just as experienced, but as expressed through the mediating operations of understanding, judgment, and decision. Later, Lonergan will speak of the "world mediated by meaning and motivated by value," where "motivated by value" pertains more precisely to the level of decision (deliberation, evaluation, decision, action). It is very difficult to remain in the world of immediacy as an adult because we are oriented to the world through these four mediating operations. For example, when one wakes up and for an instant does not know the time or place one is in, one asks oneself spontaneously, "Where am I? What day is it?" The questions emerge from within oneself, and the answer comes rapidly (one would hope!) because the mediating cognitional operations occur spontaneously. Instances in which adults return to the world of immediacy Lonergan calls "mediated return[s] to immediacy;" they are encountered in the contexts of art, philosophical interiority, psychotherapy, sexual intercourse between lovers, and mystical experience.

Efficient meaning pertains to getting things done through the recurrent, patterned exercise of attention, intelligence, reasonableness, and responsibility. The construction of a building or a roadway, for example, is a clear example of efficient meaning.

Constitutive meaning often pertains to the fundamental formalization or institutionalization of a group's values: a constitution, declaration, or mission statement, for example, defines and sets parameters that guide the mentality and behaviour of a certain community. To change or fundamentally reinterpret the constitutive meaning is to change the community. This can occur radically, in a revolution, or less dramatically, when the constitutive meaning is reinterpreted.

The *communicative* function of meaning refers to any expressions of meaning communicated from one human being to another, regardless of the medium of communication. To the extent that the communication is successful, it becomes part of the public common fund of knowledge both synchronically and diachronically. Diachronically, it becomes part of history and is subject to reinterpretation, distortion, and the like. It is important to note that biases, misinformation, and myths can also make it into the common fund of knowledge.

Constitutive and communicative meaning yield three notions: community, existence, and history. Communities form with the achievement of common meaning. Where there are different kinds of communities, a community is formed based on "a common field of experience, common understanding, common judgments and common commitments" (77).

But common meaning can be biased, and so a community, as a collection of individuals, faces the precarious human drama of authenticity versus inauthenticity. There is a minor authenticity or inauthenticity that is the challenge of an individual as related to a community or tradition. A failure of minor authenticity is a judgment upon the individual. There is also the major authenticity and inauthenticity of a tradition. Provocative here is Lonergan's suggestion that fields of knowledge, schools, and eras of thought can be distorted, "so the unauthenticity of individuals becomes the unauthenticity of a tradition. Then, in the measure a subject takes the tradition as it exists for his standard, in that measure he can do no more than authentically realize unauthenticity" (78). Given recent discussions of structural racism, this last sentence is very apropos. In structural racism, good people can participate in unjust structures, and, as the quote suggests, despite their intentions, they can be implicated or facilitate further racism.

But human beings are unique in that they have a deliberative power to create themselves and to influence and reshape their communities. Human beings are not just subject to the laws of nature. They are historical beings who can, in dramatic ways, shape their own destiny. Lonergan does not say much about history in this section. This may be because he devotes chapters 8 and 9 of *Method in Theology* to history and also because he will open to a discussion of the stages of meaning in the final sections of the chapter on meaning. "Meaning has its invariant structures and elements, but the contents in the structures are subject to cumulative development and cumulative decline" (78). All human science will need to take hermeneutics and history as basis, in large part to identify and reverse distortion and decline, as well as promote development (78).

Four Realms and "Four" Stages of Meaning[9]

Lonergan identifies four realms or "worlds" that human beings generally live in, insofar as society has differentiated these four realms. They are the worlds of *common sense*, *theory*, *interiority*, and *transcendence* (genuine religion). There are three *exigencies* that give rise to the realms respectively (systematic, critical, and transcendent), the realms being operative principally on certain differentiated levels of consciousness (groups of operations on a distinct level; i.e., common sense is to experience as theory is to understanding, as interiority is to judgment, as transcendence is to decision/commitment),[10] and the realms also being conceived of as *stages of meaning* for understanding (Western) historical developments.[11]

In draft pages of the chapter on meaning in *Method*, Lonergan stated: "The four realms of meaning [common sense, theory, interiority, and transcendence] have a dynamic aspect. They are reached only through successive differentiations of consciousness. Accordingly, they provide a basic scheme for distinguishing different stages of meaning."[12] The need for realms to emerge into various stages of meaning rests on the exigencies or needs that arise when prior realms are distinguished and permeate a society or civilization, but have been overextended, or signal the need for a further differentiation. The question emerges: if there are four distinct realms, why not four distinct stages of meaning? That is a question we will return to later, as Lonergan at least initially conceived of a fourth stage of meaning. But our answer must equally be complicated by the fact that the conception of a fourth stage of meaning he had in mind was weighted towards vertical alterity (i.e., God) rather than horizontal alterity (i.e., one's neighbour).

Each differentiation of these worlds comes about by a specific exigence or need that calls forth the distinct world, often with some resistance from the current context. As these worlds are conceived of as developments in history, we can speak of them as stages of meaning. I will explore the realms and stages together, although they make up two sections in *Method*.

Rarely does a person negotiate all four realms successfully. If there is anything today close to a so-called Renaissance man, it is a person who can navigate relatively comfortably between three or more of these various worlds. Moreover, there is no need to choose one of the worlds over another, but human bias may resist, prefer, or even reject one world over another. And, to some extent, personal interest and social opportunity may determine one's ability or preference for one world over another.

Each of the worlds arises as a need or exigence calls forth further differentiation in the ordering of human knowledge. Likewise, each world can be distinguished by how the subjects are related (1) to other things (common sense), (2) as things related to each other (theory), (3) as subjects related to themselves (interiority), or (3) as subjects related to another (transcendence).

First Stage to Second Stage

The default world is the common-sense world. Without it, we could not get out of bed in the morning. Common sense is the world that characterizes the first stage of meaning. Lonergan has a very broad understanding of common sense. It pertains to the "world" or cosmos of "things" as related to the person or community. The world of "things" as related to us is made up primarily of the world of practical affairs, of getting things done, and of the world of the drama of human relations and dealing with people. Common sense is acquired through "the self-correcting process of learning" (79), where cumulative "wisdom" is learned from experience – trial and error. But one could say it also encompasses the world of the artist, who seeks to express the world of things related to us creatively in artistic works.

When it comes to explanations for the nature of things, however, the world of common sense is limited in its ability. It can describe a tree, for example, but it cannot explain what makes a tree a tree and not a stone. In ancient Greece, the best common sense could do to explain the origins of things was through myth. The mythic explanations for things are often connected closely to the description of the object – the explanation of a tree would be connected to an account of its mythic origin. In the world of common sense, especially as undifferentiated common sense, "explanations" of the created order are provided on the basis of mythology. In this way, the transition from the first stage to the second stage of meaning begins with the Greek discovery of mind. For example, the grooves in Devil's Tower in Montana were traditionally believed by Indigenous tribes in the area to be caused by the claws of a giant mythic bear. But science will give a very different explanatory account of the grooves in Devil's Tower based on the latest geological science.[13] In the absence of other realms, common sense is undifferentiated. Still, within the various divisions of labour, specialized common sense develops (*CWL* 10, 74). For example, the various types of surgical tools are known to the surgeon easily, but not to a layperson.

The common-sense world contrasts with the realm of theory, where things are related to one another, and explanations are provided. When Thales and Heraclitus began asking what the nature of reality really is, they were acting out of the systematic need for theory that human knowledge required if it was going to advance in understanding of world processes. Here, a systematic exigence begins to emerge in Western philosophical history, one that will culminate in the second stage of meaning. This stage is where the world of theory emerges as a separate realm from common sense. The second stage finds a correlate in the emergence of modern science, but philosophically and theologically was prior to that already expressed in the systematic achievement of Aquinas's *Summa*. Science has long dismissed most of the conclusions of the Presocratics (e.g., that water or fire was the principle of all being); but the latter attempts were in a way pre-scientific or pre-explanatory. The fact they were asking the question of how "things are related to other things," however, indicates their realization that common sense is not up to the task of addressing questions about the nature of things, and that something more is needed. Human curiosity requires a consideration of the "nature" of things – in a word, the world of things related to one another.

This movement from the first (common sense) to the second stage of meaning (theory) is significant for Lonergan in that it marks the beginning of an "intellectual conversion" in the history of philosophy, insofar as Plato, as exemplified by his allegory of the cave, recognizes that knowing is "not just a matter of taking a good look" (196). The prisoners in Plato's allegory are deceived by appearances and sensible experience. Knowing involves something more than sensible experience per se: it involves an act of understanding that yields ideas, and such ideas must later be open to verification in a further cognitional operation, *judgment*, although the latter is not yet worked out for Plato. Nonetheless, the legacy of Plato is well established: the invisible world of forms or ideas is conceivably independent, in some sense, of the world of the senses.[14] The fruit of the transition from the first to the second stage of meaning is the possibility of theoretically differentiated consciousness. The latter emerges because of a systematic exigence that "separates the realm of common sense from the realm of theory" (78). Plato's overemphasis on the invisible world of the ideas bespeaks how difficult it is to properly relate the worlds of common sense and theory to one another. An oscillating tension will occur throughout the history of ideas between the empiricists and the rationalists. The uneasy balance of these two worlds calls forth the need for a third stage.

Second Stage to Third Stage

The transition from the second to the third stage of meaning comprises the shift from the data of sensible experience to the data of consciousness – the shift from the content of the operations to the operations themselves. On the surface, the shift may resemble the second stage, but it is really about objects *and* an intending subject. The shift comes about as the subject tries to make sense of two seemingly vastly different worlds: common sense and theory.

The emergence of modern science represents a differentiation between the consciousness of common sense and that of theory, so that, among other things, the task of philosophy changes. Whereas philosophy used to ask, "What is the nature of …?," this question is now asked by the sciences. The philosophers, in turn, begin to ask different questions: "How are these two realms, common sense and theory, related to each other?" Eventually, the philosopher (i.e., the birth of modern philosophy in Descartes) must turn inward to human interior consciousness in order to relate these two seemingly separate worlds in an attempt to find their common ground and unity. We can apply to this transition what Lonergan refers to as realms of meaning.[15] That is, the attempt to relate these two worlds properly emerges as the result of a *critical exigence*. The latter exigence gives rise to interiorly differentiated consciousness. The paradigmatic inauguration of this turn to the subject, or interior consciousness, occurs with Descartes's quest for an indubitable, and is further exemplified by the endeavours of Hume and Kant. However, all these brilliant attempts leave us with a legacy of scepticism and lead inevitably to what Michael Polanyi describes as a "doctrine of doubt."[16] This translates into our current philosophical context as a deep suspicion of epistemology and metaphysics (one that is somewhat understandable, but nevertheless unsustainable) by postmodern thinkers and others.

For Lonergan, the questions philosophers are now to be concerned with are: "What am I doing when I am knowing?" (cognitional theory – philosophy of mind), "Why is doing that knowing"? (epistemology), "What do I know when I do that"? (metaphysics), "What do I do with what I know?" (ethics), and "Is there a ground or term of all knowing and doing?" (philosophy of religion). Indeed, he sets out in *Insight* to reckon with the paradigmatic philosophical turn to the subject. He seeks to take its fundamental achievements as a starting point and philosophical foundation upon which to eventually construct a systematic theology in the spirit of Thomas Aquinas. The latter will be an ongoing, collaborative venture. Lonergan's intellectual context is much more complex than that of Aquinas because he must consider a plethora of philosophical, scientific, and technological achievements, and also those in the social sciences. To avoid a fragmentation of knowledge and splintered academic disciplines, he wants to explicate the unifying ground of knowledge, rooted in one's conscious interiority, which also provides a basis for grounding the plurality of positions.

The third stage of meaning begins when philosophers turn to their own conscious interiority to find an adequate ground for knowledge and metaphysics. It will culminate in the general acceptance that knowing is not just looking, but consists in the recognition that one comes to know through the cumulative, recurrent cognitional operations of *experience*, *understanding*, and *judgment*. However, if one accepts Lonergan's philosophical perspective, then one recognizes that he corrects this legacy of scepticism in that his turn to the subject establishes *the self-affirmation of the knower* and *the grasp of the virtually unconditioned* in judgment in which we can actually know (*CWL* 3, chaps. 9 and 10). The acknowledgment and affirmation that I am a knower competes as a dissenting voice in a context permeated by the doctrine of doubt, and may seem like a radical statement by comparison. "Genuine objectivity is the fruit of authentic subjectivity," as Lonergan says, where "authentic" is what makes the difference between knowing, on one hand, and subjectivism, scepticism, and relativism, on the other (273). In the third stage of meaning, metaphysics and theology have their ground in corresponding acts of cognitional operations. As for his use of "genuine," suffice it to say it requires being attentive to one's experience, intelligent in one's understanding, reasonable in one's judgments, and responsible in one's decisions. It requires a faithful adherence to one's unrestricted questioning and asking all the relevant questions in each inquiry. Equally important is Lonergan's precept to be in love: with one's family, with one's neighbour (community), and with God, which we will address in the next chapter, on religion.

For those who are reluctant to turn to interiority, for whatever reason, Lonergan assures the reader that this turn "is not an end in itself" (81). It is necessity to turn inward only to return more capably to the worlds of common sense and theory. Here, he uses the phrase "methodical exigence." The methodological exigence propels one to distinguish adequately between common sense and theory without confusing them, and simultaneously provides the comfort of a unitive base in a generalized empirical method. But it also provides a basis for analysis of the two worlds, "for self-appropriation of itself is a grasp of transcendental method, and that grasp provides one with the tools not only for an analysis of commonsense procedures but also for the differentiation of the sciences and the construction of their methods" (81).

Fourth, Lonergan identifies a transcendent exigence. Our knowledge is never complete; our curiosity always demands to know more. Our judgments rest on a virtually unconditioned, grounded by a formally unconditioned; deliberation affirms finite goodness but pines ultimately for the ground of all goodness. The transcendent exigence takes us beyond common sense, theory, and interiority, into the realm "in which God is known and loved" (81). Lonergan leaves his remarks there, stating that he will address it in the chapter on religion. I will return to the topic in relation with the fourth stage of meaning; but first, a note on "troubled" and "undifferentiated consciousness."

Development of human knowledge occurs from undifferentiated consciousness towards differentiated consciousness. However, such development can be resisted. We are part animal and so we should not be surprised if we automatically default to the world of immediacy and sensibility when confronted with questions of reality. Lonergan references Eddington's two tables, the table in relation us (common sense) as brown, having a hard surface, and so on, and the table related to other tables as possessing "wavicles," molecules, and so on. These two tables are emblematic of two different (valid) worlds. But to common sense, these new insights can be disorientating, or troubling. So Lonergan speaks of "troubled consciousness" as one becomes acquainted with this new world of theory. But troubled consciousness accompanies each differentiation, at least initially, so that the turn to interiority is resisted, as the turn to the subject is resisted, as a wrong turn. The differentiation is from common sense to self-knowledge, in the sense of the Delphic maxim "Know thyself." Troubled consciousness may eventually become more comfortable with the other worlds, but it may also become persistent in its resistance, so that aspects of undifferentiated consciousness remain even in the later stages (81).

There are several senses of undifferentiated consciousness that Lonergan is referring to, although he does not clearly delineate them. First, there is the undifferentiated consciousness of the ancient Greek world, prior to the systematic exigence that seeks to explain the nature of things, that based its views of the world on the myths of Homer rather than upon reason. Closely related to this is the undifferentiated consciousness of Aboriginal or Indigenous peoples prior to substantive encounter with the Western mentality.[17] Lonergan references Lévy-Bruhl's theory, a largely discarded theory of preliterate peoples that argued that "they do not reason logically and coherently, but poetically and metaphorically." Lévy-Bruhl's theory was dismissed, especially as anthropology moved into empirical studies, but his influence carried over into philosophy in the "comparative study of thought styles," and had an influence on hermeneutics.[18] Similarly, Lonergan likely viewed Lévy-Bruhl's theory as corroborating what he means by undifferentiated consciousness. This is not to say that preliterate peoples were not logical: Lonergan's notion of generalized empirical method presumes that all human beings are naturally rational and logical in their thinking. Rather, the undifferentiated consciousness does not neatly distinguish between common-sense and religious differentiations. In this way, Lévy-Bruhl's assertions about the natural religious orientation of preliterate peoples may be better understood not anthropologically but philosophically, as an early attempt to express undifferentiated consciousness.

Second, there is the natural progression of human development as a child is educated from the world of common-sense language to the world of theory as they progress to secondary and tertiary education. As children are educated in the different levels of consciousness, there will be a collective appropriation of interiority into the common sense of the community. But interiority has not yet been sufficiently integrated into the mainstream and has even been resisted. Frederick Crowe once mused on the future of such an integration when he imagined that one day children would be playing hopscotch on the four levels of intentional consciousness – experience, intelligence, judgment, decision.[19]

Third, undifferentiated consciousness appears in the later stages insofar as the emergence of one realm is privileged over another, or is half-heartedly blended with common sense. Common sense resists the new realms. The emergence of grammar and rhetoric as an art in ancient Greece gave rise to a form of humanism that overstated the role of language and rhetoric in human uniqueness and achievement. A privileged, educated class emerges. The moral imperative of *philanthropia* emerges, whereby humanity exercises generosity not out of a religious conviction, but out of a devotion to human beings as human beings.

Fourth, we have a blending of common sense and theory. "But it will also happen that theory fuses more with common nonsense than with common sense, to make the nonsense pretentious and, because it is common, dangerous and even disastrous" (94). Finally, the differentiation brings forth a difference in poetry. Prior to the differentiation it was exploratory; after the differentiation, one has to select the type of poetry one is going to invoke.

Lonergan's point in this section is that, as differentiation occurs throughout the Western tradition, there is resistance to further differentiations. Specifically, the world's common-sense resistance to theory is what Lonergan terms *general bias*. An elite class can develop that may or may not care to share their wealth and knowledge, so those who are said to live in an ivory tower would suffer from *an intellectualist bias*.[20]

Undifferentiated consciousness in the later stages is pervasive especially when it is passed on by the mass media and educational system. The celebration of human achievement finds its limit, not in the proliferation of humanisms, but in its inability to confront two insolvable questions: the ultimate meaning of life and the question of evil. So Lonergan's warning is ominous: "Never has adequately differentiated consciousness been more difficult to achieve. Never has the need to speak effectively to undifferentiated consciousness been greater" (95). He ends the chapter on meaning with these words. But this takes us to the threshold of the chapter on religion, and for Lonergan this will mean the introduction of grace.

For Lonergan, interiority is something very specific. It means making one's intentional operations the content of one's attention, inquiry, insight, and judgment. This achievement of interiority marks the third stage of meaning. However, since Lonergan's writing, questions remain as to what an expansion of that notion of interiority might entail. Moreover, it would seem incomplete that the whole history of ideas would culminate in interiority. Therefore, the question arises concerning the possibility of a fourth stage of meaning – one that implies self-transcendence beyond interiority and towards alterity, horizontally to others, and vertically to transcendent value. Before looking more closely at Lonergan's notion of religion in the next chapter, I turn to this question of a possible fourth stage of meaning.

Transcendence and the Fourth Stage

Lonergan did speak of a fourth stage of meaning, but did not develop it. What he had in mind has to be extrapolated from the notion of being-in-love in the chapter on religion in *Method*.[21] That notion presumes there to be a transcultural basis for genuine religion expressed as charity and self-sacrificing love within subjects; in other words, it presumes love to be the basis of genuine religion. But Lonergan was not naively optimistic: he also delineates the major distortions of genuine religion as well. Further, the fourth stage of meaning is fitting when Lonergan speaks of transcendence as a fully differentiated realm in the same text (see 248–49).

Lonergan laboured chiefly to provide a philosophical response for a third stage of meaning – the turn to conscious interiority. However, let us take some liberty and speculate what a fourth stage might entail. For example, we can ask: if the task of the third stage of meaning is the critical appropriation of one's intentional consciousness – the basic task of philosophy – what might be the comparable task of theology in a fourth stage of meaning? I will return to this question later, but first let us presume for a moment that there is a fourth stage of meaning. As we have seen, the transition from the first to the second stage of meaning is brought about by a *systematic exigence* that results in the possibility of theoretically differentiated consciousnesses, one that correlates with the level of *understanding* for Lonergan. The transition from the second to the third stage of meaning comes about as the result of a *critical exigence* so that the subject can adequately relate the seemingly disparate worlds of common sense and theory. Likewise, the turn to interiority enables the critical grounding of this relationship between common sense and theory, and further yields the possibility of interiorly differentiated consciousness. This stage can be correlated with the level of judgment for Lonergan in that this is the basic task of philosophy. That is, the philosophers' object of inquiry becomes consciousness, and their main task becomes critical reflection: to ask, "What are we doing when …?"

Admittedly, Lonergan identifies these exigencies when he speaks of the realms of meaning rather than the stages of meaning. However, they are pertinent to the stages because it is possible to locate their emergence concretely in history. For example, Descartes's *cogito* comes about as the result of a critical exigence, not just in Descartes's own intellectual questioning but insofar as Western philosophy needed it as well – he inaugurates the *Zeitgeist* of the turn to the subject.

Therefore, if we suppose that there is a fourth stage of meaning, then we can take as a clue what Lonergan refers to as a *transcendental exigence* in order to understand the emergence of that stage:

> There is to human inquiry an unrestricted demand for intelligibility. There is to human judgment a demand for the unconditioned. There is to human

deliberation a criterion that criticizes every finite good. So it is – as we shall attempt to show in the next chapter [on religion] – that [humans] can reach basic fulfillment, peace, joy, only by moving beyond the realms of common sense, theory, interiority and into the realm in which God is known and loved. (83–4)

Lonergan implies that the transcendental exigence takes us beyond realms of common sense, theory, and interiority, which are characterized by the three stages of meaning, respectively. Therefore, we can logically deduce, consonant with his mention of the other differentiations of consciousness, that the transcendental exigence gives rise to religiously differentiated consciousness – a consciousness that connotes a person who is habituated into the dynamic state of being-in-love in an unrestricted manner. In this way, we can surmise that a fourth stage of meaning would bring about an emphasis on religiously differentiated consciousness, including a generally heightened desire for a basic fulfilment as transcendent. As we will see in the next chapter, this unrestricted being-in-love *is* the basic fulfilment for which all human beings long, whether their conscious intending occurs in the world of common sense, theory, interiority, or some combination thereof. It is the *basic* fulfilment; but I presume Lonergan chose his words carefully, so we can assume it is not the complete fulfilment. Such fulfilment would pertain to the finality of human longing for the beatific vision.

Much of what Lonergan says about unrestricted being-in-love pertains to what he identifies in religious conversion. The latter concerns a transformation such that one's being becomes a dynamic state of *being-in-love*. There follows a desire to surrender and commit to that love, which has a content but no apprehended object.

> Religious conversion is being grasped by ultimate concern. It is otherworldly falling in love. It is total and permanent self-surrender without conditions, qualifications, reservations. But it is such a surrender, not as an act, but as a dynamic state that is prior to and principle of subsequent acts. It is revealed in retrospect as an under-tow of existential consciousness, as a fated acceptance of a vocation to holiness, as perhaps an increasing simplicity and passivity in prayer. It is interpreted differently in the context of different religious traditions. For Christians it is God's love flooding our hearts through the Holy Spirit given us. (240–1)

In this way, we can surmise that, where interiority provides the conditions for the self-appropriation of the human person to affirm himself or herself as a knower at the level of judgment, being-in-love in an unrestricted manner implies the affirmation of a transcendent Other. This, in turn, demands a commitment and self-surrender, a constitutive act like the choice Ignatius calls for in the *Two Standards*. So a fourth stage of meaning would correspond to the level of decision, the way in which interiority corresponds to the level of judgment – but with the qualification that it reflects the subject's commitment that flows from the dynamic state of being in love.

Moreover, unrestricted being-in-love is not just a recognition of a transcendent Other, of whom one is conscious, but does not know: it also includes the love that flows over into one's family and one's neighbour, and leads to a general desire to contribute to the well-being of humankind. In his later writings, Lonergan often speaks of religious conversion in the context of family, of society, and of God. We can derive from this that the fruits of unrestricted loving include not just a vertical recognition of and response to a transcendent Other, but also a horizontal recognition of and response to the other – family, friends, neighbours, society, and, perhaps most importantly, one's enemies.

As unrestricted loving demands complete and total self-surrender, the fruits of such self-surrender entail a complete reordering and reorientation of one's knowing and choosing. In terms of knowing, the realms of common sense, theory, and interiority are reoriented and redirected in line with this unrestricted being-in-love. In terms of choosing, one commits oneself to self-surrender in light of this basic horizon of loving. One comes to the resolve that being attentive to one's experience, being intelligent in one's understanding and reasonable in one's judgments – not restricting the unrestricted desire to know – is the responsible and loving way in which to act. Moreover, one accepts responsibility for one's neighbour; one chooses to love one's enemy. Nor is this the sole prerogative of Christianity, as the Dalai Lama demonstrates in his ongoing non-violent response to the Chinese government.

The fourth stage of meaning is characterized by a new way of multireligious interrelationality beyond the distortions, rivalries, and violence of deviated transcendence. It emphasizes a critical appropriation of one's faith tradition and an ecclesiology of friendship, mutuality, dialogue, and discernment as its presuppositions. It anticipates, with Robley Whitson's *Coming Convergence of World Religions*, not a convergence of doctrines per se but of renewed cooperation, not simply out of practical necessity but in a spirit of charity.[22] The fourth stage of meaning anticipates a collective stage of development, in a similar spirit as James Fowler's final stage of religious development – universalizing faith.[23] However, this speaks to the issue of vertical alterity insofar as the multireligious cooperators together orient themselves collectively towards transcendence. The fourth stage of meaning would bring with it a renewal of horizontal alterity, a priority given to one's family, neighbour, and community through the universal values of love and justice, including a preferential option for the poor and marginalized. In short, it is a collective and explicit twofold turn to alterity: horizontally, towards one's neighbour, and vertically, towards ultimate transcendent value (God). However, the vertical alterity, functioning as a kind of first principle, elevates and places the horizontal alterity in its proper orientation – relating human beings to one another and collectively towards transcendent value. Among other things, it anticipates a stage in human history (paradoxically inaugurated in the past century) of integral ecumenical relations among the world's religions. I do not have space to rehearse what I have said in other essays about the characteristics of the fourth stage of meaning; suffice it to say that it brings with it a priority given to and a promotion of dialogue and community, and a critical appropriation of one's own faith tradition as a sign of mature faith. It also focuses upon mutuality, dialogue, discernment, and friendship as methods of engagement with the other.

Although her own differentiations would have been within common sense and religiously differentiated consciousness, the mystical life and spirituality of Catherine of Siena provides an allegory for the differences between the third and fourth stages of meaning. Consider that, for Lonergan, the self-affirmation of the knower, a pivotal point in intellectual conversion, is precisely a positive statement: "Yes, I am a knower." By contrast, in the mystical life of Catherine, self-knowledge is by way of negation: God tells her, "I am he who is, you are she who is not." This is to say that self-knowledge beyond the world of interiority and in the religiously differentiated realm shifts to acknowledge the existence of a transcendent Other. To extend the allegory, Catherine had been living in a virtually hermetic seclusion when Jesus, her mystical spouse, tells her that she must now go out into the world to be of service. Jolted out of her hermetic life, she becomes a force for ecclesiastical reform, an authentic Christian witness in service to others.[24] This allegorical description of her life, albeit imperfect (she did petition for a crusade against the Muslims, at one point), reflects how interiority, when fueled by the supernatural aspect of the transcendent exigence (a graced falling in love with God), opens up to love for others – horizontal alterity. This engagement with transcendent value reinvigorates, renews and reconditions one's relations with others. One does not just fall in love with God: one falls in love with those whom God loves.[25] Horizontal alterity is inextricably related to vertical alterity for Christians because the immanent Trinity is fundamentally relational, and the offer of God's grace makes it possible for human beings to participate mystically and intimately in those immanent divine relations.

The self-affirmation of the knower in the world of interiority brings him or her back to the world of common sense, to the world of concrete living, with its human relations and practical intelligence. I would note here that the emphasis on vertical and horizontal alterity as flowing from a proper self-appropriation of one's interiority, facilitated by a transcendent exigence, can provide a defence against the concerns of thinkers – such as Hans Urs von Balthasar – who are suspicious of the turn to the subject. One cannot avoid interiority – those theologians who keep to Aquinas, as von Balthasar does, are right to do so, insofar as Aquinas offers a theological achievement for the second stage of meaning; however, they fall short of meeting what Lonergan, following José Ortega y Gasset, called "the level of the times."[26] The achievement of Aquinas has to be transposed into interiority – otherwise the Thomists remain in a museum of sorts, relishing the heights of the second stage of meaning (see 317).

Apart from the general risk of taking a "wrong turn" in the turn to the subject, as pointed out earlier, interiority may trouble integralists more particularly because it demands self-reflection. Lonergan once suggested, in one of his letters, that the Ignatian examination of conscience should now be considered an examination of consciousness more generally.[27] While I would not label von Balthasar an integralist, I am suggesting that there is an intellectual bias that can obstruct the progress of theology in the third stage of meaning by a resistance to the interiority and self-reflection required by that stage. Distinct from the third stage, theology in the fourth stage of meaning will be inter-religious. Comparative theologians have already come to this conclusion, but their specialized methods have not sufficiently met the methodical exigence; consequently, they have little to say about the ultimate goal of comparative theology, or its role in a broader constructive or systematic theology.[28]

The rationale for a fourth stage of meaning follows from what Lonergan refers to as the *transcendental exigence* in *Method*. This exigence speaks to the conscious intending that ultimately leads our inquiring, a desire for unrestricted intelligibility, truth, and goodness and, with its goal, basic fulfilment in transcendent value (God). This occurs "only by moving beyond the realms of common sense, theory, and interiority and into the realm in which God is known and loved" (81). Moreover, it is clear that the transcendent exigence leads to a distinct differentiated realm – one that objectifies the gift of God's love as expounded in chapter 4, on religion (249). Presumably, this includes horizontal alterity, whereby "human subjects are concerned with themselves and with one another" (*CWL* 16, 153).

The Fourth Stage: Some Questions

Again, at least initially, Lonergan *does* use the terminology of a fourth stage: "The third stage results from meeting the critical and the methodical exigences, and the fourth [religion] adds an adequate apprehension of the transcendent. The third and fourth stages are those that would result inasmuch as transcendental method and its application to natural science, human science, philosophy, and theology become accepted."[29] He continues: "The third stage results from meeting the critical and methodical exigences. Its characteristics have been, perhaps, sufficiently indicated in this and the foregoing chapters. The nature of the fourth stage will be indicated in the next chapter [on religion]."[30] So, while it is clear that Lonergan had used the term "fourth stage," it is unclear why he did not continue to use it. As I asked before, if there are four distinct realms, why would there not also be four distinct stages of meaning? Allow me to speculate as to why Lonergan did not stay with the language of a "fourth stage."

The first reason could be that Bruno Snell's work *The Discovery of the Mind: The Greek Origins of European Thought*,[31] which Lonergan uses at least for the transition from the first to the second stages of meaning, does not really account for religion. While it also fails to address the transition to the third stage of meaning, Snell's chapter 10, on "the origin of scientific thought," does outline the context for what Lonergan identifies as the critical and methodical exigences to emerge. Religion or spirituality comes into play in the final chapter of Snell's book, which addresses Virgil's *Eclogues*, but it is a notion of religion that is still undifferentiated from common sense and myth. Such a conception of religion can be an impediment to the advance towards subsequent stages, as when Galileo's challenges to the biblical accounts of creation incensed the ecclesiastical authorities of his day because the latter had taken the biblical accounts for "common sense," and the former's theories called that assumption into question.

What Lonergan has in mind in his notion of religion is that the fourth realm, *transcendence* (i.e., "genuine" religion), comprises a fully differentiated level of its own, along with common sense, theory, and interiority (248–9). I will unpack the significance of this in more detail in the next chapter; for now, suffice it to say that an implication of what Lonergan has in mind is that the transcendent exigence does not simply orient the entire cognitional and volitional structure towards ultimate fulfilment in God: the transcendent exigence also gives rise to a transcendent realm fully differentiated in the cognitional structure, along with the full differentiation of the other three realms – common sense, theory, and interiority. Ideally, the realms, as manifested in history, comprise the respective stages of meaning.

This leads to the second reason Lonergan may not have stayed with the language of a fourth stage: a fourth stage, as he conceived it at that point, did not sufficiently account for horizontal alterity – being in love with other people. This is complicated, however, by his cursory treatment of the methodical exigence (the application of transcendental method to common sense and theory), which fails to explicate how horizontal alterity pertains to dramatic living. Lonergan's reference to the methodical exigence applies to common sense, to be sure, where dramatic living with others is a vital component; but his example of common sense implies generalized empirical method as an application of practical intelligence in the common-sense world, and its application to the development of theory in scientific discovery (see 81). Presumably, generalized empirical method equips people to deal with others in all aspects of their living. But falling in love with another person takes one out of oneself, so the reference to alterity, which needs to be explicated in terms of the methodical exigence, also needs to be clarified in the special case of people falling in love, and also that of the elevation of that love, when one falls in love with God unrestrictedly. That is, the transcendental exigence in Lonergan's view primarily focuses on vertical alterity (i.e., relationships with God); hence, just as the critical exigence gives rise to the realm of interiority, the transcendent exigence goes beyond this interiority to alterity, something Lonergan does not explicitly state, but does imply in *Method*. In chapter 4 of *Method*, Lonergan focuses primarily on this alterity as a relationship of falling and being in love with God. He acknowledges that the best analogy for understanding this dynamic state of being in love with God is that of two human beings who fall in love (109); but his emphasis in chapter 4 is nonetheless on vertical alterity (relationship with God), without sufficiently differentiating horizontal alterity, or relating it to vertical alterity. He concedes that there are other types of being in love than being in love with God: there is romantic-spousal love, the love between parents and children, and philanthropic love – love for the broader community or nation, or the world (101).

Here the question arises: what kind of intelligibility and value is the primary concern for the fourth stage of meaning? In the world of common sense, the questions for practical intelligence are only concerned with objects as related to the subject or community. The world of common sense alone as undifferentiated concerns the first stage of meaning. By contrast, the world of theory is concerned with the world of things as related to one another; as such, the realm that arises from this theoretical differentiation on the second level of intentional consciousness unfolds in history as a second stage of meaning. The third stage of meaning arises through the critical and methodical exigences. It is *critical* because it gives rise to the need to relate the worlds of common sense and theory to one another – the turn from objects to operations in one's consciousness. It is a *methodical* exigence because it compels the subject to relate these seemingly disparate worlds to one another through the subject's interiority by relating cognitional operations to one another (experience-understanding-judgment-decision). The fruit of such self-appropriation is the ability to apply generalized empirical method explicitly to any discipline, field, or situation.

Now, if common sense relates things to oneself, theory relates things to one another, and interiority relates conscious operations within the subject to one another, what would be the equivalent for the realm of transcendence? In terms of horizontal alterity, it would be human beings as subjects related to each other as subjects (not as objects). In an essay entitled "The Ongoing Genesis of Methods," Lonergan writes that "besides the dialectic that is concerned with human subjects as objects, there is the dialectic in which human subjects are concerned with themselves and with one another. In that case dialectic becomes dialogue" (*CWL* 16, 153). The ready example that comes to Lonergan's mind is ecumenical and multifaith dialogues, insofar as these involve authentic subjects who may differ on their respective conceptions of transcendence. However, the realm of transcendence does more than seek to relate subjects to other subjects: presumably, the fruit of interfaith dialogue would be to address the relation of subjects to a transcendent subject or ground of all value, which is construed differently in different faith traditions. The last quotation from Lonergan is unique in that it emphasizes horizontal alterity, whereas, in general, Lonergan tends to emphasize vertical alterity in the realm of transcendence. In any case, the two alterities are intimately related, and stand in need of further filling out.

Horizontal alterity in fully differentiated consciousness would function as a *minor* fruit of the transcendent exigence, just as being in love with someone is to grasp the ontic value of that person (it takes one out of oneself) – the *me* becomes a *we*. By contrast, the *major* fruit of the exigence is the dynamic state of being in love in an unrestricted manner with the ground of all value.[32] Horizontal alterity and its role in self-transcendence has been the subject of scholarship on Lonergan in more recent years, both in the argument for a fourth stage of meaning and in discussions around a fifth level of consciousness (which Lonergan also acknowledges) – in addition to the various recent attempts to put Lonergan in discussion with Girard and Levinas.[33]

Finally, it may be that Lonergan's inability to sufficiently clarify the differences between the so-called natural examples of being in love (spousal, parental, philanthropic love) and what one might call "supernatural being in love" (the dynamic state of being in love in an unrestricted manner) occasioned his discarding of the language of a fourth stage of meaning.

The transcendent exigence raises the question of whether there is a ground of knowing and doing that is ultimate truth, goodness, and beauty. Among other things, the transcendent exigence propels the subject out of the world of interiority and into the world of common sense (as well as theory) with a renewed vigour for human relations and human well-being. The transcendent exigence is not content for human beings to know and to do in particular instances: rather, it brings forth an anticipation of the fulfilment of all our knowing and doing that is partially fulfilled when people fall in love. As long as one is in love, that love is the most important aspect of one's lives. We can speak of being in love horizontally, with other human beings, and vertically, with God. Lonergan devotes the chapter on religion in *Method* to the latter.

One should note that it is not only the internal transcendent exigence that demands cooperation among the world's religions in our time. There is, further, an external exigence that would facilitate and perhaps expedite the emergence of a fourth stage of meaning. For the first time in human history, the technology to inflict mass casualties, and even to destroy humanity entirely, exists. The need for genuine dialogue and civil modes of discourse has never been greater. In Lonergan's chapter on religion, he seeks to provide a basis for common dialogue, which could answer to this need; we turn our attention now to that chapter.

5 Lonergan's Notion of "Genuine" Religion

Lonergan's chapter on religion in *Method in Theology* is one of the key chapters in this ground-breaking work. In addition to its placement alongside chapters on philosophical method (chapter 1), the human good or value (chapter 2), and meaning (chapter 3), the fourth chapter, on religion, is at once (1) an expansion, extrapolation, and transposition of his early work on operative and cooperative grace in Aquinas, (2) a universal and normative claim for the existence of a transcendent ground of value, set in a language that, at least for its time, aims to invoke a wider, ecumenical, and neutral nomenclature, (3) an exposition of the basis – namely, this just-mentioned transcendent ground of value, which is integral to his method in theology – from which special theological categories will be derived, (4) a theory of genuine religion, and, along with it, (5) a corresponding theory of distorted or destructive religion – a theory about the dialectical nature of religious development. It should also be mentioned that certain implications of the thought in this chapter can provide a context for an emerging integral relatedness between the world's major religions as part of what I have called a fourth stage of meaning. However, at this point in Lonergan's career, having suffered a bout of cancer and lost a lung, he likely did not have time to develop the nuances and sophistication that he would have liked to, as he did in works such as *Insight*[1] and his two-volume theology of the Trinity.[2] His priority in writing *Method* was to communicate the varied and ordered functional specialization. However, much in the work remains to be commented upon, qualified, and developed.

Elsewhere, I have suggested that the foreground chapters on meaning, the human good, and religion express Lonergan's expansion and complexification, as he worked it out in *Insight*, of Kierkegaard's three existential spheres of the aesthetic, the ethical, and the religious, respectively – although Lonergan would not view them as stages.[3]

Moreover, in contrast to Kierkegaard's treatment of the religious sphere, which necessitates that one become a Christian, Lonergan's treatment of religion is more universalist and does not demand that one be a Christian, although it does advocate authenticity, of which we will say more later.

Lonergan begins the chapter talking about the question of God, self-transcendence, and religious experience. This will provide the basis for his (1) universalist notion of religion, (2) notion of genuine religion, and (3) delineation of distortions of such religion.[4]

In his lectures on method in Dublin (1971), Lonergan outlined the structure of the chapter at hand in terms of grace. He first considers "the room in us for grace," likely referring to the sections on the question of God and self-transcendence. Then he treats "the nature of the experience of grace" in the section on religious experience. Next, he deals with "the distribution of grace" in the section on the expressions of religious experience, extending God's grace to other religions. Finally, he addresses "the relation of grace to faith" and "the relation of faith and beliefs."[5] Clearly, Lonergan's notion of religion is inextricably related to his understanding of grace, which also formed the basis of his early thought.[6] What Lonergan did not include in those comments is a section on the dialectical nature of religious development addressing the refusal of God's grace.

The Question of God

The reality of evil that confronts human beings will inevitably raise the question of ultimate transcendence. Each of the three levels of intentional consciousness – understanding, judgment, and deliberation – in whose respective limits different types of questions emerge, inevitably raises the question of God. Questions for intelligence will ultimately lead to questions about the intelligibility of the universe as a whole. This in turn leads to the question of whether there is an intelligent ground – God. Reflection about questions for judgment will eventually raise the question of a ground for the certainty of our judgments. Questioning the ground of conditioned judgments whose conditions have been fulfilled leads to the question of an unconditioned – God. Of course, the question can be put in different ways: one can ask whether a necessary being exists to ground all contingent beings, or one can ask if there is some reality that transcends this world.

In deliberation, one can ask whether deliberating is worthwhile at all. This is to ask about the basic meaning of existence. Lonergan asks: "But is the universe on our side, or are we just gamblers …?" (98). The existentialist philosopher Albert Camus famously asked: "Why not just commit suicide?" In a sense, Camus was asking the question whether deliberating was worthwhile, although in a different manner, of course.[7]

"In the measure that we advert to our own questioning and proceed to question it, there arises the question of God" (98). For Lonergan, the question of God cannot be avoided. Atheists have asked the question enough to reject it outright, and agnostics have asked the question enough to remain non-committal. But for Lonergan, it is natural that questions anticipate answers; so, if our whole intentional consciousness is based on questioning, might we anticipate an affirmative answer to the question of an ultimate ground?

Self-Transcendence

By "self-transcendence" Lonergan does not mean that we literally transcend ourselves, but rather that we are naturally oriented towards growing and expanding our personal horizons intellectually, rationally, and deliberately. There is a perennial, existential tension within us between who we are in this moment and who we are to become. Self-transcendence leads us to grow along this trajectory. A human being "achieves authenticity in self-transcendence" (100). One of the things that sets human beings apart from the animals is our intelligence and unlimited inquiring. We are not just confronted by the field of our experience: we ask questions about it, we reflect and judge. Moreover, our self-transcendence is not just from experience to understanding to judgment, but also to *doing*, and so it is moral and constitutive. "The transcendental notions, that is, our questions for intelligence, for reflection and for deliberation, constitute our capacity for self-transcendence" (100). To the extent that we stop asking these questions, we stop growing spiritually.

Moreover, our self-transcendence moves from a capacity to an actuality when we fall in love. Its occasion, and the corresponding commitment that follows, reflect one's being in love. Such love gives meaning and purpose to our lives, and guides our decisions for as long as we remain in love. Lonergan identifies three kinds of love: familial love, philanthropic love, and ultimate transcendence – God.

Lonergan does not elaborate on the first two kinds of love, but focuses rather on being in love with God in the rest of the chapter. He writes:

> As the question of God is implicit in all our questioning, so being in love with God is the basic fulfilment of our conscious intentionality. That fulfilment brings a deep-set joy that can remain despite humiliation, failure, privation, pain, betrayal, desertion. That fulfilment brings a radical peace,

the peace that the world cannot give. That fulfilment bears fruit in a love of one's neighbor that strives mightily to bring about the kingdom of God on this earth. (101)

Note the implication: every time we inquire, we are ultimately asking about God, since all truth and goodness have God as their source. Love of God perdures despite obstacles; it is a source of internal strength and resilience. Note too that his terminology as seen earlier does not specify God as the answer, but God as the basic fulfilment. Love of God gives our inquiring for knowledge and direction a basic orientation and meaning that subsequently direct our interests. In a word, we do not stop asking questions once we fall in love with God: rather, our inquiring takes on its proper orientation, that orientation for which it was intended. Thirdly, note that he refers to being in love with God as the *basic* fulfilment of our conscious intentionality, and not the complete fulfilment. His reference to the reign of God suggests that complete fulfilment is anticipated eschatologically.

The fruit of the loves is charity towards people; cumulatively, this love contributes to advancing the reign of God's love on earth. What I have called, in the previous chapter, the fourth stage of meaning entails the clarification of horizontal alterity, elevated through a sustained encounter with the vertical alterity of God's love. This fourth stage of meaning is a further instantiation and explication of the advancing reign of God on earth. In addition, the basis for genuine religion Lonergan is arguing for in this chapter implies that the advancing reign of God will be inter-religious, an integral, ongoing engagement with cultural and religious pluralism.

A Note on Kierkegaard and the Negative Aesthetic

Lonergan states: "The absence of that fulfilment (of being-in-love) opens the way to the trivialization of human life in the pursuit of fun, to the harshness of human life arising from the ruthless exercise of power, to despair about human welfare springing from the conviction that the universe is absurd" (101).

So Lonergan identifies three results of the absence of the fulfilment: hedonism, abuse of power, and despair consequent on a belief in the absurdity of the universe. Interestingly, Kierkegaard's aesthetic sphere has three progressions that correspond to these three results Lonergan mentions. The type for the first progression is Don Juan, who represents the hedonic flight from the anxiety of existence in his adventures seducing many women. The second progression is represented by Faust.

Rather than seducing many, Faust focuses on a total domination of one, Gretchen: it is power that motivates him, rather than the escapist pleasure of a Don Juan. Finally, the third progression, represented by the legend of Ahasuerus, the wandering Jew, expresses despair at an empty, aimless existence.[8]

This destructive progression in Kierkegaard's aesthetic sphere inspired von Balthasar's severe criticism of Kierkegaard, blaming him for separating the aesthetic and ethical spheres, and hence contributing to the loss of beauty.[9] I have responded elsewhere, from a Lonerganian perspective, to von Balthasar's criticism. Here I simply wish to point out that to the extent that von Balthasar's criticism of Kierkegaard's negative aesthetic is indicative of the loss of beauty, then being-in-love with God, as a basic fulfilment, would be a solution to the recovery of beauty for which von Balthasar so passionately argues.[10]

Religious Experience

Lonergan distinguishes between being-in-love with God, as experienced, and its thematization into categories, at the level of understanding and judgment. Being in love with God is being in love in "an unrestricted fashion" (101). As long as this love lasts, it is a state, and it is the most important realty in our lives. Once the falling in love occurs, it guides all our knowing and choosing thereafter. Appropriating a notion of Nietzsche's, Lonergan describes this transformation as a "transvaluation of values." The previous values we had do not disappear, but are re-ordered in light of this new situation, with the transcendent value being the most significant priority.

This state is the fulfilment of our questioning and desires, but not the "product" of our knowing and choosing. It is a gift, which Lonergan describes in language of the second stage of meaning as sanctifying grace. Sanctifying grace is the grace of justification rooted in the soul that gives rise to the habit of charity, making people capable of disproportionate acts of love. He also refers to this dynamic state as operative grace, the grace from which habits, or cooperative grace, emerge. Lonergan cites Saint Paul to list the fruits of being in love in this manner: they are "acts of kindness, goodness, fidelity, gentleness, and self-control" (102; see Gal. 5:22–3).[11] By these fruits, one can discern whether one is in love with God.

Being in love with God is conscious on the fourth level, deliberation. This means that we grasp the value and significance of our state, but we do not "know" it in the sense of a compound of experience, understanding, and judgment. Moses knew he had encountered tremendous value when he encountered the burning bush, but he had very little idea with whom he was communicating. As conscious but not known we experience the gift as a mystery. Because it is a state of being in love, we experience it as "not just attractive but [as] fascinating" (102). We are compelled by this unknown from the depths of our being. Since we experience the mystery as unplumbed depths and power, it evokes awe in us.

But Lonergan is not concerned yet with the assignment of the gifts of God's love to theoretical categories such as sanctifying grace. In this chapter, he is speaking of that love mainly as religious experience. Subsequent classification is the task of systematics. Further, because it is an experience that can be known by its fruits, the question of the existence of this experience in other religions arises (103). Lonergan assumes that "God is good and gives to all [human beings] sufficient grace for salvation" (105).

Expressions of Religious Experience

Lonergan's presumption when speaking about religious experience is that it is positive, so that one could place the adjective "genuine" before "religious experience" – where "genuine" refers to the experience as it "spontaneously manifests itself in changed attitudes" reflective of "love, joy, peace, [patience,] kindness, goodness, fidelity, gentleness, and self-control" (104). Lonergan is not naive, however: he is aware of the possibility of distorted notions of religious experience, which he addresses in the next section of the chapter. As a Jesuit who has undergone extensive formation in the *Spiritual Exercises* of Saint Ignatius, he also presumes that genuine religious experience will be discerned precisely by those fruits listed by Saint Paul (see Gal. 5:22–3). Moreover, the interpretation of such religious experience will vary according to the stages of meaning.

In the first stage of meaning, religious experience is associated with the distinct time and place of the hierophany – manifestation of the divine. The multiplication of and resemblance among hierophanies can be construed as polytheism. The perception of a unity undergirding the various instances of religious experience of a community leads to monotheism, although Lonergan does not use that word. In the second stage of meaning, religious experience is expressed theoretically in terms of grace, and with the assistance of a mediation from outside the tradition. In the case of Aquinas, for example, the philosophy of Aristotle provided such mediation. Such expressions are exemplified in the medieval notion of sanctifying grace and the habit of charity.

Of course, temptations beset each of these stages. In the first stage, there is the belief that one can *make* one's relationship with the divine. One may be concerned to appease, or at least not to offend, the gods by means of a ritual system. In the second stage, there is the temptation to excessive theoretical abstraction, which distances one from the originating experience.

In the third stage of meaning, Lonergan presumes that genuine religious experience is akin to falling in love as the initial or deepening of a dynamic state of being in love with God. The importance of the third stage is that, by construing religious experience in terms of interiority, one can relate the first and second stages in such a way as to keep the concreteness of the earlier stage, while also enriching it with the understanding from the second, theoretical stage – which can guide a renewed praxis. However, as we will see, there is a need to further thematize the commitment that flows from the dynamic state into a subsequent stage, accounting for alterity and hedging against the risk of an overemphasis on interiority or a temptation towards navel-gazing.

Frederick E. Crowe, one of the foremost commentators on Lonergan, points out that Lonergan arrives at his religious universalism by two approaches: one, theological, relying on the letters of Saint Paul (especially 1 Tim. 2, 4 and 1 Cor. 13) as its sources; the other, empirical, drawing from the historiography of religions of his day.[12] I begin with the empirical approach, although the methods of the study of religion have changed and developed since Lonergan's reading in the field.[13] Lonergan was intrigued and influenced by Friedrich Heiler's classification of seven areas of commonality among the major world religions.[14] We see that the former's notion of being-in-love in an unrestricted manner, which is the basis of his notion of genuine religion, is directly influenced by Heiler's thought here. Lonergan summarizes Heiler's seven principles of commonality as follows:

(1) "that there is a transcendent reality";
(2) "that [the transcendent reality] is immanent in human hearts";
(3) "that [the transcendent reality] is supreme beauty, truth, righteousness, goodness";
(4) "that [the transcendent reality] is love, mercy, compassion";
(5) "that the way to [the transcendent reality] is repentance, self-denial, prayer";
(6) "that the way is love of one's neighbor, even of one's enemies"; and
(7) "that the way is love of God, so that bliss is conceived as knowledge of God, union with [God], or dissolution into [God]." (105)[15]

Lonergan asserts that the seven areas of commonality are implicit in what he refers to as "the experience of being in love in an unrestricted manner" (105). This claim of his can be justified if we notice the near one-to-one correspondence between the structure Lonergan outlines that defines unrestricted being-in-love, and Heiler's seven commonalities. Lonergan describes the structure of unrestricted being-in-love as follows:

(1) it is being in love with a transcendent "someone,";
(2) who is "in my heart, real to me from within me";
(3) that someone is "supreme intelligence, truth, goodness";[16] and
(4) "he himself must be love";
(5) "it is also a denial of the self to be transcended"; "it is prayer, meditation, contemplation";
(6) this love "overflows into love of all those that he loves or might love"; and
(7) finally, it is characterized by a "longing for union," the "bliss of knowledge of him and union with him." (105–6)

Approaches like Heiler's have fallen out of favour as the study of religion has become much more empirically restricted in its methodology. Claims to universality are resisted, among other reasons, out of a fear of not accounting sufficiently for the differences between different religions. To enter methodological debates in the study of religion would be beyond the scope of this book. However, one wonders: if biologists can come to certain agreements about commonalities in human anatomy and physiology, why would there not be commonalities among human religious experiences and values? After all, the Christian, the Muslim, and the Hindu are not members of different species, but human beings who for a complex of reasons have adopted, over history, different expressions of answers to the ultimate questions of transcendent value.

The second approach Lonergan takes to a universalist notion of religion is more explicitly theological. He presumes that God's grace is universally offered to all people, regardless of race and religion. However, this does not mean that everyone will accept it. Lonergan often alludes to 1 Timothy 2:4, where God wills the salvation of everyone; while it is implicit in *Method* (see 105), he cites it explicitly in other works.[17] The implication of the passage from 1 Timothy is that if God wills something, sooner or later, being all-powerful, it will happen. I will not go into the implications of such an assumption for universalism – which von Balthasar has raised anew in our era – because Lonergan did not address eschatology much. In another place, Lonergan takes the sufficiency of salvation signified by the presence of charity in the heart of the believer to be discernable according to 1 Corinthians 13:13. God "gives all [human beings] the gift of his love, and so it further follows that there can be an element in all the religions of [hu]mankind that is at once profound and holy" (*CWL* 17, 170). In *Method*, too, he talks about the transcultural aspect of the gift of God's love. The gift of God's love is not comprehended; it is experienced as content "without apprehended object." So at its base in experience, and as a dynamic state, it is transcultural – "that object will be conceived differently in different cultures. But if you haven't got an apprehended object, if it is just the content of being in love, then it can be transcultural" (265n20). How is one to know whether the gift of God's love is being authentically expressed in a cultural or religious context? Again, Lonergan cites Saint Paul, claiming that the gift of God's love will be known through its fruits (see Gal. 5:22–3): "Though not the product of our knowing and choosing, it [the fulfilment] is a conscious dynamic state of love, joy, peace, [patience] that manifests itself in acts of kindness, goodness, fidelity, gentleness, and self-control" (102). While the gift is offered freely, the manifestation of the state in acts of charity is an unmistakable sign that the gift has been accepted. In the context of inter-religious dialogue, this means, among other things, that the fruits of the gift of God's love can and should be discerned in light of the criteria of Galatians 5:22–3.

There is evidence that love is at the heart of the genuine expressions of all the world's religions. To give a few examples: in Judaism, there is the foundational prayer of the Shema; in Christianity, there is the Johannine and Pauline emphasis on love (e.g., John 15:13; 1 Cor. 13:13); in Buddhism, there is an emphasis on compassion, love, and equanimity; and in the Muslim religion, as argued by William Chittick, there is the centrality of love and mercy.[18] In Judaism, Christianity, and Islam, in particular, the emphasis on love would be in contradistinction to the popular view that religion is primarily about following rules (that is, it is reducible to ethics), and the overemphasis on transcendence to the point of a bifurcation between the created order and God's self-communication. Moreover, it is to give love priority over truth. This is not to demote the importance of truth; but, at least where the Christian religion is concerned, truth would pertain to revealed knowledge in faith, while faith, Saint Paul tells us, does not have the same status as love – keeping in mind, however, that the statement, "The greatest of these is love" (1 Cor. 13:13) is itself a revealed truth for Christians.

Here it should also be emphasized that, in *Method*, Lonergan is talking as a Christian theologian to other Christians. This said, however, if God's love is universally given and manifests itself in other religions, then Saint Paul's criteria in Galatians 5:22–3 are to be the discernible signs for what Lonergan understands to be genuine religion. But the best way to gain clarity on what Lonergan means by genuine religion is to look at his thought on *distortions* of genuine religion, which lead to degeneration and violence.

Religious Development Is Dialectical: Distortions of Religion

In the next section of the chapter on religion, following the seven common traits of the major religions and those of the dynamic state of being in love in an unrestricted manner, Lonergan treats "religious development [as] dialectical." Here he acknowledges a dialectical tension between genuine religious expression and its corresponding distortions. "The dialectical character of religious development implies that the seven common areas or features will be matched in the history of religions by their opposites" (106). The distortions are made explicit here:

1. An overemphasis on transcendence leads to no personal dimension of God; or, there is a distant impersonal God controlling the universe.
2. An overemphasis on immanence leads to idolatry, magic, and myth.
3. A denial of any ultimate ground of truth, goodness, and beauty: in his words, "easily reinforced by erotic, sexual, orgiastic."
4. Awe and respect for God become terror of God.
5 and 6.   Love of neighbour and self-denial become hatred of others and oneself.
7. Conceptions of God "slip over into the demonic"; the effect on human beings is "destructiveness of oneself and of others" (106–7).

This list is not exhaustive of religious aberrations, but rather provides a sketch. Among other things, the work of René Girard on religious violence could contribute further to this theory. The mixture of genuine religion with its corresponding distortions is a perennial problem for the religions of humankind (106). Indeed, the seven distortions occasioned an earlier argument by this author that understands evil as a mimicked distortion of the good; I have analysed this thesis elsewhere in connection with Girard and Lonergan.[19]

Lonergan's understanding of the dialectical nature of religious development can be further enriched if we posit a *dialectic of religious identity*. Within explicitly religious subjects and communities, there is a dialectic between two foci: on one hand, the *specific-identity-focused*, who understand their religious identity by distinguishing themselves from the other, and on the other, the *general-identity-focused*, who emphasize their commonality with the other. Moreover, there are genuine and inauthentic expressions of each of these foci. Positions will, of course, fall on a spectrum; but in terms of the extremes, we have the inauthentic specific-identity-focused, such as those who attempt to impose their beliefs on others, with varying degrees of coercion, and the inauthentic general-identity-focused, who risk losing or surrendering their identity in an accommodationist manner. In addition, there are those extraordinary persons, whom Louis Massignon describes as "the elite," who can integrate the best of the genuine specific and general identity foci.[20] One can think of James Fowler's stage six of psychological religious development – *universalizing faith*, as demonstrated by Thomas Merton and others.[21]

Lonergan would likely agree with the contention that anti-religious sentiment in our day is fueled by the inauthentic distortions of religious identity: compromise, on one hand, and hatred and violence in the name of religion, on the other. Conversely, the genuine religious expressions that flow from true love and self-sacrifice for the other are to be the redemption of religion from its distortions. Lonergan states: "Genuine religion is discovered and realized by redemption from the many traps of religious aberration" (106). But genuine religion must be discerned, and that discernment is to occur within individual believers, when they critically appropriate their own faith tradition rather than view it as simply a set of rules to follow, like a logical deduction from premises to conclusion. It must be a discernment of one's own tradition and the various biases and distortions that may reside there. It must be a discernment of the different kinds of differences – complementary, contradictory, and developmental – one may encounter when faced with the other. Finally, it must be a discernment that favours an *intra-religious* form of dialogue, following Raimondo Panikkar, whereby one reflects on one's faith as a result of listening to the religious other, in order to integrate fruitful insights.[22]

Lonergan's theory of the dialectical notion of religious development is not comprehensive; rather, as we have seen, it parallels Heiler's seven commonalities among the world's religions. More could be said on the topic of distortions, but the work of René Girard will suffice as a supplement to what Lonergan is doing here. Girard discusses at length deviated transcendence, whereby religion is co-opted in acts of violence against the innocent.

The Word

By "the word" Lonergan does not mean the specific theological meaning ascribed to Jesus Christ, the incarnate Son of God. Rather, he means it more philosophically, as the expression of religious experience. In other words, he means the effable attempts by human beings to express the ineffable, although only insofar as the ineffable can be understood.

There is a prior word that is unexpressed in the immediacy of religious experience. Insofar as this immediacy is expressed, it is so through the mediation of meaning in "outer words." But the outer word is subject to the limitations of language, and is conditioned by the historical context of that language. Nonetheless, the outer word is important and necessary; this is because it has a constitutive function: without the testimony of the first witnesses, for example, the Christians would have had no one to follow. The word of tradition perpetuates the originating experience for subsequent generations, drawing them into and helping them name their experiences of immediacy in ever new contexts.

The outer word is also personal: the mediated immediacy expressed in words speaks to the hearts of others. It awakens them to the existential value issuing from spoken words that resonate with experiences in the depths of their being. Insofar as this affects groups of people one can say the outer word is also social. Finally, the outer word is historical, and so context becomes relevant to understanding its meaning. With respect to Christianity, this is the basis for inculturation. But it also means that knowledge of the realms and stages of meaning will be important to understanding the outer word.

Each of the four realms – common sense, theory, interiority, and transcendence – mediates the immediate experience according to their respective mode. Common sense is concerned with expression, usually through image, symbol, metaphor, and affect. Theory expresses the mystery in intellectual categories and doctrine, albeit in a limited manner. Interiority negotiates the "strange contrast and tension" between the starkly different worlds of common sense and theory. Identifying the unity in consciousness of the different worlds is the distinctive task of interiority. "For only through the realm of interiority can differentiated consciousness understand itself and so explain the nature and the complementary purposes of different patterns of cognitional activity" (111). Foundationally, expressing the outer word will entail deriving "its basic terms and relationships, its method ... from the realm of interiority" (110).

Faith

"Faith is knowledge born of religious love" (111). It is the "inward ground for religious commitment" (*CWL* 16, 54). But what does Lonergan mean by "faith"? In Kierkegaard, for example, faith is a leap when one has reached the limits of reason. We are not accustomed to thinking of faith as a knowledge. A footnote in the text (footnote 29) clarifies Lonergan's position. Faith speaks to the prior judgments (of credibility) that ground belief – the conviction in which religious beliefs arise. In *Method*, Lonergan invokes Pascal's "reasons of the heart which reason does not know." "Reason" refers to the compound of the first three levels (experience, understanding, and judgment). The "heart" refers to the grasp of value in the fourth-level operations. "By the heart I understand the subject on the fourth, existential level of intentional consciousness and in the dynamic state of being in love" (112). Consider that Teresa of Avila believed in Jesus, but through her faith, in a certain manner she "knew" Jesus – try to convince her otherwise! She knew Jesus through faith, not through natural reason. By "faith," Lonergan is referring to "another kind of knowledge reached through the discernment of value and the judgments of value of a person in love" (112).

Faith occurs in the apprehension of transcendent value (he also calls it "religious value" earlier in the book) achieved in feelings. The feelings apprehend transcendent value from an experience of basic fulfilment. But this apprehension also demands a response – a total commitment by the person. Although Lonergan calls it a "decision," it is really a commitment that will orient subsequent decisions. What Lonergan has in mind here is something like the election in the Ignatian *Spiritual Exercises*. Relatively speaking, faith "places all other values in the light and the shadow of transcendent value." Absolutely speaking, faith apprehends transcendent value as "supreme and incomparable" (112).

The knowledge of faith introduces us to the solution to the problem of human limitations and evil: "it is not argument but religious faith that will liberate human reasonableness from its ideological prisons" (114). The acts of charity (the responses) that flow from religious faith transform "human possessiveness and human pride" through the "charity of the suffering servant, by sacrificing love," and through humility. Repentance and conversion are life-long processes (114).

Religious Belief

Whereas faith is an originating judgment of value that flows from a "genuine experience," religious beliefs are the subsequent judgments of fact and value that a community affirms as derivative from and expressive of their common experience. However, as the community is made up of various individuals, the beliefs will differ as regards expression, context, development, and so on.

Nonetheless, Lonergan mentions four ways in which religious beliefs can be expressed or practiced differently. (1) The religious belief can be expressed in an "imperative … to love God above all things and … one's neighbor as oneself." (2) "It may be narrative, the story of community's origins and development." (3) "It may be ascetic and mystical, teaching the way to total otherworldly love and warning against pitfalls on the journey." And (4) "it may be theoretical, teaching the wisdom, the goodness, the power of God, and manifesting his intentions and his purposes" (114).

Although Lonergan does not explicate it in this manner, we can roughly correlate these four ways with the four worlds of commons sense (origin story), theory (theoretical), interiority (mystical and ascetical), and religious (love of God and neighbour). He then goes on to say that it can be a compound of any of these, or it can be a balanced synthesis of the four, or it can take one as basic and interpret the others in light of it. One might consider here the founding charisms of various religious orders throughout the church's history.

As communities survive and grow, they become historical in a general sense insofar as their religions endure, influencing society continuously and leaving their mark. But Lonergan has a deeper sense of the historical in mind: "The dynamic state of being in love has the character of a response. It is an answer to a divine initiative." "Genuine" religion is the response to God's "personal entrance … into history, a communication of God to his people, the advent of God's word into the world of religious expression" (115). This expression recounts the history of a people's receiving the gift of God's love and responding in kind "to love unrestrictedly, with all one's heart and all one's soul and all one's mind and all one's strength" (115). For Lonergan, the interior experience of falling in love with God can be genuine to a greater or lesser degree, and its outer expression, which becomes a tradition in a community, will be as genuine as the interior experiences at its source (see *CWL* 16, 54). As for the interior experience, so too the outer expression is measurable and discernable through its fruits (see Matt. 7:20).

Lonergan concludes that religious expression is not "just the objectification of the gift of God's love; in a privileged area it also is specific meaning, the word of God himself" (115). It is not altogether clear what Lonergan means by "in a privileged area" and "the word of God himself." One might be tempted to read this as referring to the Christian community and the person of Jesus Christ, respectively. But Lonergan does not elaborate. He simply leaves it as a theological question to be addressed by theologians.

Next, Lonergan elaborates on the value of the distinction between faith and beliefs. This distinction secures a basis for the interfaith dialogue based on religious experience. "Beliefs do differ, but behind this difference there is a deeper unity." The editors of *CWL* 14 inserted a quotation (note 31) from Lonergan's Regis College (1961) Method lectures where he qualifies that "the difference [between faith and beliefs] is important." Faith is the "eye of religious love" that can help "discern God's self-disclosures" (115). In the dialogue of religious experience, one can discern the genuine fruits of the Spirit and the seeds of the Word. But Lonergan has told us that faith is knowledge, and here he uses an optical analogy to describe faith's role in discerning beliefs. The use of the optical analogy might confuse some given that, for Lonergan, it is often used in his critiques of the myth of knowing as "taking a good look." Here, I presume he means that faith is capable of perceiving the genuine basis for general belief – although it must be discerned, and that will entail the use of experience, understanding, judgment, and decision.

Technical Note

In the final section of this chapter, Lonergan makes some important points that have significant qualification of other points he has made.

First, Lonergan has established four realms of meaning (common sense, theory, interiority, and transcendence). He is writing in the third stage of meaning where interiority is necessary to negotiate the tensions between common sense and theory. Medieval theology represented the second stage of meaning and so was theoretical. This contrasted with the Christian authors of the first stage of meaning, who attempted to articulate religious experience primarily through symbolic language. But the latter type of language does not lend itself to precision, and so calls forth the need for more precise technical distinctions proper to the world of theory. Theory lends clarity to the world of common sense, but not in such a way as to negate common sense. In fact, the two are complementary. Specialized common sense as the world related to us (*priora quod nos*) can describe the phases of the moon. By contrast, relating the phases to one another can provide explanatory understanding: namely, it leads to the discovery that the moon is a sphere (*priora quod se*). This distinction applies to religious experience. Common sense will describe the religious experience in symbol and metaphor; theory will go further, relating the similar experiences to one another to derive the notion of sanctifying grace. However, now that we have shifted to the third stage of meaning, one begins with the religious or inner experience (as related to us). The world of theory serves to name this state as sanctifying grace, so that one understands that the experience, insofar as it initiates a state, is the condition wherein one is saved. In terms of interiority, a genuine religious experience (and it is genuine insofar as it is corroborated by the fruits listed in Galatians 5:13) is identified as the state (of consciousness) of being in love without restrictions.

There are further advantages to using interiority as the basis for theology. It allows one to get beyond some of the problems resulting from the limits of the second stage, such as debates about the relations between metaphysical terminology and difficulties in articulating the proper relations between intellect and will. Lonergan's four levels of intentional consciousness operate in a dynamic unity. The fourth level, decision, guides the intellective process because we must choose to be "attentive or inattentive in experiencing, … intelligent or unintelligent in our investigations, … reasonable or unreasonable in our judgments" (117). This means two notions from the medieval legacy "vanish": (1) the notion of the pure intellect or reason, the belief that the intellect can operate independently of the fourth level, and (2) the notion of the will as "arbitrary." For Lonergan, aside from children and minors, the notion of an arbitrary will is another form of inauthenticity in that it presumes that one can be free from responsibility in one's decisions. The point Lonergan is emphasizing is that the pursuit of understanding, truth, and goodness requires a prior fundamental choice to adhere to the precepts that lead the way through the challenges of cognitive and moral self-transcendence. "A life of pure intellect or pure reason without the control of deliberation, evaluation, responsible choice is something less than the life of a psychopath" (117).

Next, Lonergan makes a technical distinction about love and the four levels, relating to the Latin adage *nihil amatum nisi praecognitum*[23] (knowledge precedes love). In the normal course of operations, this would mean that the fourth level presupposes and complements "corresponding operations on the other three" levels (117). Falling in love represents an exception to this process. It is an exception because one grasps the value of being in love before one "knows" cognitively what is really happening. However, Lonergan speaks of a minor and a major exception to this principle of knowledge preceding love. The first is that of two people falling in love. Their falling in love is "disproportionate to its causes, conditions, occasions, antecedents" (117). For example, consider all the relationships that a person has in a lifetime: a very small number of those relationships would likely comprise "falling in love." It is disproportionate in the cause and conditions of the relationship relative to the other relationships and events in one's life. Falling in love is often a life-transforming event that leads to a reordering of one's priorities and commitment to the other – a commitment that establishes a horizon of other commitments. More could be said about human beings falling in love, but the point is that the value they initially experience in the event of falling in love precedes their knowledge of what is happening.[24] "People in love have not reasoned themselves into being in love (118)."[25]

The major exception to our Latin tag is that of someone who genuinely falls in love with God or transcendent value. Whereas two human beings in love with each other know the object of their mutual love, to be in love with God is not to know with whom we are in love. "But who it is we love is neither given nor as yet understood" (118). "The person in love with God is in love, but they don't know with whom" (119n37).

Since the gift of God's love is offered to all, and the explication of this idea is integrated into Christian attitudes, a new ecumenical context is here to stay. But it also means that the task of Christian apologetics has changed. It is now not to produce the dynamic state of being in love with God (i.e., to convert people), nor to justify God's gift. "Only God can give the gift, and the gift is self-justifying." Rather, the role of the apologist is now something more like that of a spiritual director, helping people integrate God's love into every aspect of their lives (118). The apologists will help with the proper naming and interpretation of the dynamic state of being in love.

Finally, Lonergan clarifies his distinction between faith and belief. What he means by "faith" is more precisely what grounds belief, what was previously meant by *lumen gratiae, lumen fidei*, and infused wisdom. The shift to an empirical notion of culture means that there will be a need for a new understanding of the former distinctions, and such can develop without jettisoning the ancient truths embodied in the previous language (12).

In the final section, I return to the discussion of the fourth stage of meaning, a direction I believe Lonergan was heading in, since the habituated integration of the dynamic state of being in love comprises a differentiated realm. This differentiation enables one to see the world through the value of religious loving, so that one can apprehend the other in love, as when Thomas Merton states: "When you meet your neighbor, Christ meets Christ."

Genuine Religion and the Fourth Stage as a Differentiated Realm[26]

The fourth stage of meaning is concerned with vertical and horizontal relations with the divine and others. The two are intertwined. To love God is to love one's neighbour; to love one's neighbour is to love God. Responsibility in love flows over into an understanding of interrelationality, not only with others, but with the created order.

The fourth stage of meaning would not only be one propelled by a transcendent exigence, but also one that emerges from the point of view of intentional consciousness as a differentiation of transcendence as a distinct realm. As the cumulative effects of this differentiation emerge collectively, the fourth stage of meaning would be further instantiated within vertical and horizontal alterity, and bear fruit in elevated social and political relationships globally.

When Lonergan first introduces the notion of the transcendent exigence in *Method*, one might get the impression that the exigence is the univocal thrust of the other exigences (systematic, critical, and methodical), as human knowing and choosing perpetually unfold towards self-transcendence, and as a continual withdrawal from inauthenticity towards authenticity. While this is the case to some extent, at a closer inspection one will see that Lonergan has genuine religion in mind as a distinct realm to complement the differentiated realms of common sense, theory, and interiority (81). Later in the book, Lonergan acknowledges that that his comments on "transcendence as a differentiated realm have been fragmentary" (248). While his brief comments that follow this admission do not necessarily resolve the fragmentation, he does gives us a clue for filling out what he means.

He views genuine religion as the objectification of the gift of God's love "as itself a differentiated realm." But what does this differentiated realm entail? His answer to this question is twofold: first, it enables the subject to withdraw from the realms of common sense, theory, and interiority into contemplation and prayer, and second, it enables one to return to the objectifications of the gift that occur in the previous three realms, with the effect of "intensifying, purifying, clarifying the objectifications referring to the transcendent" (249). I suspect a genuine experience such as this is what von Balthasar had in mind as foundational for theologians when he said theology should be done on one's knees. Pope Francis has added: "on one's knees *and with an open mind.*"[27]

Together, these ideas express Lonergan's idea of religion as a differentiated realm capable of clarifying and improving the other realms of common sense, theory, and interiority. In terms of Lonergan's theory of intentional consciousness, common sense correlates with the level of experience, since it is for the most part, though not exclusively, about practical intelligence and human relations in the concrete world of everyday living and sensitive experience as related to the subject. In and of itself, common sense is unreflective – in Plato's philosophy, it is the world of the particular. Theory correlates with Lonergan's notion of the second level of understanding – Plato's world of ideas – although, with the birth of science, theory aims directly to discover the immanent laws in the created order, beginning its inquiry with the data of sense and returning to them for a corroboration of theory. The world of interiority correlates with the level of judgment because it brings a critical eye to bear upon ideas and theories. Lonergan was fond of saying that good ideas are a dime a dozen, implying that truly good ideas have undergone the scrutiny of judgment. Interiority also calls for a judgment when one enquires into the nature of one's own knowing. The exigence is critical in the sense that the data of consciousness (i.e., conscious operations), as opposed to the data of sense, become the locus of inquiry. The judgment that issues forth, assuming one has properly understood one's conscious operations, is a self-affirmation of the knower. But religious experience is also objectified in one's interiority.

Now Lonergan explicitly states that being in love in an unrestricted manner is conscious on the fourth level, decision (103). Hence, as a differentiated realm, genuine religion correlates with this same fourth level. I will qualify this statement shortly because it involves a discussion of the fifth level. First, how does he understand this consciousness of the fourth level? Presumably it would be a consciousness not just of value in the scale of values, but of the *ground* of value – God. Moses may not have had a very clear understanding of whom he was speaking with when he encountered the burning bush ("I Am Who Am"); but he was certain he had encountered value – indeed, the ground of value for him and his people. The dynamic state is conscious on the fourth level in that one apprehends that this is the most significant value in one's life, although one cannot comprehend it. In the scale of values, this would comprise religious value (32–3); but it would seem to include a grasp of the value that is the very ground of the preferential scale as well. The analogous but disproportionate notion of falling in love with another human being would be personal value.[28] When two people fall in love with each other, there is a commitment to each other that follows from their being in love – a reorganization of their lives, a transvaluation of values. They have not "reasoned themselves" into being in love: they just act on their love, presumably because they grasp a basic value in the other person (118). While our decisions reflect our values, our commitments reflect whom and what we value the most. But human beings can fail each other. Lovers can bring great meaning to each other; but they do not complete each other. In the case of being in love with God, it becomes the base (*apex animae*, "the apex of the soul") from which all desire for knowledge and all choices will flow (103). Being in love with God becomes the most important thing in one's life, and, at the same time, the source of basic fulfilment. Positing the fifth level is necessary because it adds to the fourth level the orientation via genuine commitment of all one's decisions in accordance with the dynamic state of being in love.[29] It seems clear in Lonergan's paper titled "Religious Commitment" that what he means by genuine religious commitment is inextricable from being in love in an unrestricted manner.[30]

The emergence of transcendence as a differentiated realm will go hand in hand with the emergence of the fourth stage of meaning. I believe this view fits well with Lonergan's comments in a public lecture where he called for a new sacralization to be fostered. This would be in contrast with the "old" sacralization, which fused religion and state, and must be dropped (*CWL* 17, 270–5). The new sacralization to be fostered would include a transformation of culture and a higher integration of interreligious and multifaith relatedness.

Finally, the emergence of transcendence as a differentiated realm would promote an integration on the fourth level of operations between withdrawal (contemplation), on one hand, and action, on the other. One need only look at the history of the emergence of religious orders in the Christian tradition for examples. Following the transformation of Benedictine styles of monastic life that brought forth the mendicants, and then again in the nineteenth century with the surge of apostolic orders, Christian spirituality has grappled with a dialectic between contemplation and action. For Lonergan, this dialectic is to be worked out on the fourth level of operations, decision. At the fourth level, one can either rest in repose, on one hand, or act, on the other.

Perhaps we have seen the seeds of this higher integration of transcendence, a differentiated realm in history reflecting the fourth stage of meaning, in Fowler's theory of religious development as universalist faith. Individuals such as Gandhi, the Dalai Lama, and Thomas Merton who have grasped the essence of their respective traditions have, in so doing, genuinely incorporated insights from other traditions into their own traditions. Merton himself seemed to be on to something like a universalist notion of religion in his discussion of the Persian psychoanalyst Reza Arasteh's notion of final integration.[31] Are these individuals historical singularities, or are they pioneers paving the way for subsequent generations that will foster a new sacralization, one not de facto antithetical to secularization, but rather that has transcended the negation of the religious other? Merton claims that the way of final integration is not "the privilege of a few": rather, "it is now becoming a need and aspiration of humanity as a whole."[32] In this way, one can say that Merton's and Arasteh's intuitions anticipated what Lonergan at least initially conceived, but did not follow up on, as a fourth stage of meaning.

6 Ordered Wisdom:
The Eight Functional Specialties

I begin this chapter by repeating the quotation that led off the introduction: "Vital, intelligent, reasonable, responsible, *mine* and Catholic[!]" These words reflect Lonergan's delight in his insight into the eightfold functional specialties. In many ways, it was the climax of his career, and chapter 5 of *Method*, which articulates this insight, forms the pinnacle of the five background chapters of that work. That chapter will also be the subject of the concluding chapter of this book, which has set out to comment on the first part of *Method*.

The emergence of modern science and history has brought with it an increasing specialization of methods and fields of investigation. One can lose sight of the forest for the trees: there is the risk of fragmentation of knowledge as the various specialists can become progressively incapable of talking with each other. Lonergan's breakthrough to functional specialties offers an alternative to this trend by articulating a methodological structure that can unite the various branches of theology. While he is speaking primarily about theology, he later admits that the eightfold structure is applicable to all disciplines of knowledge.

Lonergan writes of three types of specialization, the eight functional specialties, and, finally, the dynamic unity between the eight.

Three Types of Specialization

Lonergan introduces three types of specialization: field, subject, and functional. Field specialization results from divisions and subdivisions within the field of data "to be investigated." As the data within a field accumulate and specialties are further subdivided, it becomes difficult for specialists to comment outside of their area of concentration. An inevitable consequence is "to make the specialist one who knows more and more about less and less" (122).

By contrast, subject or department specialization is divided on the basis of the results of investigations. Field specialization focuses on "material parts," while subject specialization focuses on the "conceptual classification that distinguishes the departments of a faculty and the subjects taught in a department" (122).

"Functional specialization distinguishes and separates [eight] successive stages in the process from data to results" (122). Lonergan uses two examples to demonstrate. The first example pertains to the functional specialties history, interpretation, and research; the second, to the functional specialties systematics and communications. With respect to the first example, the schema would look like this:

History:	What multiple experts say about a given period of time
Interpretation:	The interpreter says what the text means
Research:	A textual critic presents the data, what a text says

With respect to the second example the schema would look like this:

| Systematics: | Develops theory |
| Communications: | Experiments/practical applications |

For the second example, we would not expect the systematic theologian necessarily to have the pastoral skills of a pastoral minister. Conversely, if the ministers are not guided by an adequate theology, those to whom they minister will suffer the consequences.

The eight functional specialties are interdependent and interrelated with one another. The earlier functions complement and are presupposed by the later ones. From a methodological perspective, the unity in the process is secure, while the distinct stages in the process are clarified from beginning to end. The advantage of functional specialization is that it does not preclude the other two types of specialization: "it provides an orderly link between field specialization, based on the division of data, and subject specialization, based on a classification of results." It can also "counterbalance the endless divisions of field specialization" (122).

It goes without saying that a scholar can operate in several functional specialties in any given project or investigation.

An Eightfold Division

The eightfold division of functional specialties admits of a further division into two phases, the first phase comprising research, interpretation, history, and dialectic, and the second, foundations, doctrines, systematics, and communications. Lonergan proceeds with a brief overview of each specialty; he dedicates a chapter to each one in the second part of the book, the exception being history, to which he dedicates two chapters.

Research makes data available. It can be special or general. Special research addresses a specific question, such as original doctoral research. General research makes data available more broadly – to the human fund of knowledge. Special research is dependent upon general research, although it also contributes to the expanding breadth of general research. Writing in the late 1960s and early 1970s, Lonergan seems almost to have anticipated the age of the internet with his comment: "Someday, perhaps, [general research] will give us a complete information retrieval system" (123). We are certainly closer to achieving this in the digital age, with various search engines and electronic databases.

Research makes data available, while *interpretation* seeks to understand what the data mean. Scholars must learn the common-sense context of the community from which the texts they interpret arise. Interpretation, also known as *hermeneutics*, is where things can go awry as regards contemporary philosophical problems surrounding truth and perspectival approaches. The way that lawyers can massage facts with rhetorical skill is an example of how interpretation can claim too much for itself.

History is divided into basic, special, and general history. Basic history deals with facts and events of specific periods and places. Special histories deal with cultural, institutional, or doctrinal movements. General history is that which all historians strive for and contribute to in their own research. It is the ideal of a "total view" resulting from the cumulative results of all historians. All three have their place in the functional specialty history, since the church historian is concerned with facts, historical movements, and the broader relations between Christianity and other churches, or Christianity's relations with other religions and its role in "world history" (124).

Dialectic deals with differences in various viewpoints. It particularly is concerned with conflicts and getting to the root of them. The latter entails an investigation of differences that are irreducible or contradictory, those that are complementary, and those that contribute to a larger development. Among those differences that are irreducible or contradictory, dialectic chooses which ones are the most serious, and signals the ones lacking in psychological,[1] intellectual, moral, and/or religious conversion. In sum, "by dialectic, then, is understood a generalized apologetic conducted in an ecumenical spirit, aiming ultimately at a comprehensive viewpoint, and proceeding towards that goal by acknowledging differences, seeking their grounds real and apparent, and eliminating superfluous oppositions" (125).

Foundations focuses first and foremost on the "objectification of conversion." Lonergan's emphasis here is paradigmatic for several reasons, but primarily because foundations' starting point is the opposite of that of the older fundamental theology, which was deductive and began with doctrines. The older paradigm was concerned with the true religion (*de vera religione*), the divine law (*de legato divino*), the church (*de ecclesia*), biblical inspiration (*de inspiratione scripturae*), and the sources of theology (*de locis theologicis*). One of the questions that arises from this paradigm shift is what role these aspects of the former fundamental theology should play in the new. Are they to be discarded, or are they to be reinterpreted in terms of the priority of the thematization of the subject's religious horizon? And if they are to be retained or reappropriated, as the case may be, is ecclesiology to be addressed in foundations, or more properly in the functional specialty systematics, or both? These questions remain to be answered.

Foundations, as Lonergan conceives it, makes the horizon of theologians the basis upon which doctrines are to be apprehended. The extent to which that horizon is genuinely converted is the extent to which the horizon can authentically apprehend or express doctrines.

Conversion is a profound about-face in someone's personal horizon. It effects a change in outlook, values, decisions, and commitments. It is private, but its effects are social. Conversion can occur in dramatic instances, or it can be prolonged and more gradual. It can happen to an individual, or a collective, which may in turn form a community. The understanding and articulation (objectification and thematization) of that common experience is the narrative of a community's origins. Historically, the *ecclesia* in this new schema is an *ecclesia ex hominibus* that shares a common transformative experience of God's love in Christ, and perpetuates it down through the generations.

But what does Lonergan mean by "conversion"? He does not elaborate in this section, but rather speaks of it in subsequent chapters. It is worth mentioning the three conversions here and saying something about a fourth psychological conversion.

By "conversion," Lonergan does not mean anything having to do with one's external religious affiliation; rather, he has in mind an intellectual, moral, and religious conversion of one's personal interior horizon. Intellectually, it pertains to the transformation of one's belief from the myth that knowing is "taking a good look" to the apprehension and judgment in one's own consciousness that knowing is a compound of experience, understanding, and judgment (223).

Lonergan states in the Regis College Lectures on Method that intellectual conversion "distinguishes the world of immediacy and the world mediated by meaning" (225n8). Moral conversion transforms the basis for one's decisions from satisfaction to value. In a word, it is perhaps illustrated in the practice of delayed gratification, discussed by M. Scott Peck in his book *The Road Less Traveled*. However, moral conversion is an ongoing process: "one has to keep scrutinizing one's intentional responses to values and their implicit scales of preference" (226). Religious conversion, as Lonergan points out in the chapter on religion, is a commitment that flows from the dynamic state of being in love in an unrestricted manner.

As we have seen, and as has been generally accepted by Lonergan and his followers, there is a need to clarify the psychological transformation of the subject's personal horizon. Whereas intellectual, moral, and religious conversion assists in healing the threefold bias (individual, group, and general bias) (226), there is a need for the healing of dramatic bias as well. Dramatic bias does not have the same moral implications as the other biases, since the subject cannot always be held morally culpable for the psychological wounds they have suffered. Moreover, as Doran has pointed out, psychological self-transcendence pivots on the healing of the repressive censor that prevents people from accessing data and images that might lead to insight.[2] In fact, Lonergan admits as much when he states that conversion "releases the symbols that penetrate to the depths of [the] psyche" (126). However, there is likely a repressive censor operative in other forms of bias that prevents one from attending to relevant data that might subvert the bias.

"*Doctrines* express judgments of fact and judgments of value" (emphasis added). They are not just confined to ecclesiastical pronouncements, but exist in all the branches of theology so that there are methodological doctrines to guide research, theory, and practice. The doctrines "stand within the horizon of foundations," and are to be properly understood in the context of the previous five functional specialties (127). As well, the functional specialty communications will be the context in which questions arise concerning the proper understanding of doctrines.

Systematics seeks to understand the doctrines. The need for understanding arises because doctrinal expressions can vary according to different types of language, thus leaving them open to misunderstanding. Working against this risk, systematics "is concerned to work out appropriate systems of conceptualization, to remove apparent inconsistencies, to move towards some grasp of spiritual matters both from their own inner coherence and from the analogies offered by more familiar human experience" (127).

"*Communications* is concerned with theology in its external relations" (127; emphasis added). Lonergan mentions three kinds of such relations, which we can label *dialogue, inculturation* or *contextualization,* and *adaptation*. Dialogue is to be interdisciplinary, crossing all branches of human knowledge, and is to engage other religions.[3] Inculturation broadly entails a transposition of the Christian faith into the contemporary situation. The challenge here is to navigate the old and the new – to retain religious identity and enrich it through a critical appropriation of both the old and the new. Adaptation refers to theology's need to adapt to changes and developments in media and technology.

One might wonder if this functional specialty is the Lonerganian equivalent of traditional pastoral theology and spirituality. In brief, the functional specialty communications is "applied theology," so there is a role here for practical theology. In the chapter on communications, which we will not go into detail on here, Lonergan references Rahner's multivolume *Handbuch der Pastoraltheologie* as a model for this functional specialty. So we can presume that the traditional topics assigned to pastoral (or practical) theology remain in communications, which perhaps could more aptly be named *praxis* – Lonergan says as much (130). Spirituality, however, which often falls under applied specialties in pastoral or practical theology departments and seminaries, would likely find its analogue in the functional specialty foundations. This is because the study of spirituality is useful for exploring foundational religious experiences and discerning the difference between authentic and inauthentic conversion.

Finally, it goes without saying that communication should be two-way. Lonergan presumes this, but does not specify that the functional specialty communications is a two-way process, or, as we pointed out in chapter 1, that the church's relationship with the other is one of mutual-self mediation – where each enriches, complements, and challenges the other.

Grounds of the Division

The eightfold functional specialties can be divided according to two principles of division. First, there is a division into two phases. The first phase Lonergan refers to as *in oratione obliqua* (indirect speech); it involves the first four functional specialties (research, interpretation, history, and dialectic). The second phase he refers to as *in oratione recta* (direct speech); it involves the latter four functional specialties (foundations, doctrines, systematics, and communications). In a word, the first phase confronts the past, and the second phase confronts the contemporary situation with a view towards the future.

The second principle of division relates each of the functional specialties to a particular level of consciousness, based on the goal of the specialty. The interpreter of a text has as her goal interpretation – to *understand* what an author meant. This does not mean that the interpreter does not invoke the other levels of consciousness; rather, while functioning as an interpreter, she will be guided by the goal of the functional specialty interpretation, which is to understand, and which, as her goal, will prescribe the parameters of her investigation. However, systematics also has understanding as a goal, though in a different way than interpretation: the systematic theologian seeks to understand the mysteries of the faith insofar as they can be understood by human reason.

The goal of history is to make judgments. One might think that the goal of history is to present the facts of the past. Without going into too much detail, the two chapters on history see facts as judgments. So, there is a sense in which the historian's job is to collect facts as judgments upon events in history. However, there are many facts, and a historian is bound to be overwhelmed by the data. Therefore, the judgments that historians make pertain more importantly to the key turning points and developments. In other words, they judge what is going forward in a specific community, context, or era. For example, imagine you are writing an autobiography. In deciding how to divide and arrange the various aspects of your life history, you would make specific judgments. You would not be so much concerned with relating routines as with relating specific, critical movements and developments in your life. Historians take an analogous approach when they make judgments concerning the histories of particular groups of people.

The eightfold schema and the two principles of the division can be expressed as in figure 6.1.

The second phase of specialties are in inverted order from the first phase. Lonergan explains:

> In the first phase one begins from the data and moves through meanings and facts towards personal encounter. In the second phase one begins from reflection on authentic conversion, employs it as the horizon within which doctrines are to be apprehended and an understanding of their content sought, and finally moves to a creative exploration of communications differentiated according to media, according to classes of [human beings], and according to common cultural interests. (130)

128   The Wisdom of Order

	First phase (mediating the past)		Second phase (mediated to the future)
	Dialectic	Decision	Foundations
	History	Judgment	Doctrines
	Interpretation	Understanding	Systematics
	Research	Experience	Communications

Figure 6.1. The eight functional specialties in relation to the four levels of consciousness and the two movements (discovery and teaching)

The Need for the Division

Lonergan is not creating these functional specialties *ex nihilo*: rather, he is improving upon and appropriating previous categories: foundations, doctrines, systematics, and communications are recast from the former fundamental, dogmatic, speculative, and pastoral theologies, respectively.

Research recasts textual criticism and other kinds of research. Interpretation recasts commentaries, interpretive monographs, and the like. History recasts church history, dogmatic history, historical theology, and *Heilsgeschicte*. Apologetics is taken over by dialectic.

Lonergan emphasizes that the operation distinctive to each specialty is part of one single process from data to results. The various branches are not to be understood as distinct operations. It should be noted as well that a scholar is not limited to one of the specialties, but may make a home in one and yet branch out into others, as the line of inquiry she pursues may require. But why is this reorganization necessary? Lonergan gives four reasons:

1. There is need for a reorganization due to the fragmentation of knowledge. The distinction is of specialties, not specialists. The focus on the specialties arises so that the specialties are not confused with one another.
2. The eight tasks have eight corresponding ends. If one does not know them, one can get confused, drifting into another specialty without realizing it, and stunting one's results.
3. The eightfold distinction is needed to "curb one-sided totalitarian ambitions," or the illusory belief ("blind spot") that one specialty is better than another. By contrast, the eight functional specialties offer "a well-reasoned total view" (131).

4. The distinction is needed to "resist excessive demands." A scholar need not excel in all eight specialties. But one can hope to contribute to one specialty, and such an operation would have two parts: (1) the major part would be the production of work proper to the specialty in question, and (2) the minor part would be the scholar's awareness of the parameters of the specialty within which she operates, which would help in the overall clarification of her process. In other words, a scholar can contribute to her specialty, and her awareness of the limits of her specialty will improve the quality of her contribution.

Dynamic Unity

The unity brought about by this process is a dynamic, not a static, one. "Development, then, seems to be from an initial state of undifferentiation through a process of differentiation and specialization towards a goal in which the differentiated specialties function as an integrated unity" (132).

Lonergan gives some examples of the differentiation of development, the first one being how the Christian religion and theology are gradually distinguished. Second, the division occurs in theology itself. Field specialization emerges and eventually encompasses the matter of the first phase (research, interpretation, history, and dialectic), while subject specialization encompasses the second phase (foundations, doctrines, systematics, and communications).

With respect to the four specialties of the first phase, the unity is not logical in the way that conclusions are deduced from premises; rather, each specialty addresses "successive partial objects in the cumulative process that inquiry promotes from" the recurring sequence of the four levels of operations (experience, understanding, judgment, and decision) (134). Consequently, the structure is not closed, but rather is open, given that new data and questions can emerge along with a deeper understanding, critical refinement, and dialectical engagement with the data, as discoveries are made and contexts change.

The functional specialties are dynamically interdependent through a "reciprocal dependence" (134). This means that each specialty depends on the previous one, with the prior specialty providing the basis for the subsequent one. For example, dialectic depends upon research, interpretation, and history, but dialectic provides "heuristic structures" (cognitional theory) that can in turn guide the method of research, interpretation, and history. Because the functional specialties interlock, it will be nearly impossible for one researcher to master them all, and so teamwork will be in order.

The first phase "ascends" from data to "interpretative, then to a narrative, then to a dialectical unity." The second phase "descends from the unity of a grounding horizon towards the almost endlessly varied sensibilities, mentalities, interests, and tastes" of humankind. Again, it is not a logical deduction, but "a succession of transpositions to ever more determinant contexts" (135).

The four specialties in the second phase (foundations, doctrines, systematics, and communications) are interdependent in the same manner as the first four.[4] For example, systematics guides communications with good theory, but communications raises questions that push systematics towards a renewed understanding and even a revisitation of doctrines. Moreover, the four specialties of the second phase are guided by orthopathy (foundations), orthodoxy (doctrines), ortho-theory (systematics), and ortho-praxis (communications). Lonergan does not use this language, but it is appropriate in guiding the ideal for each specialty. Noteworthy is the notion of orthopathy (right disposition) to guide foundations. As we stated earlier, the extent to which the subject's personal horizon is converted psychologically, intellectually, morally, or religiously is the extent to which they will be well disposed for developing categories and explicating doctrine properly.

The question naturally arises whether there is an interdependence between the first and second phases. Lonergan answers yes, but with a qualification: the second phase must not dictate or dominate the first phase. That would lead to obscurantism of discourse in the second phase. Such a dynamic, it may be argued, characterized the pre-Vatican II church, prompting the calls by Pope John XXIII to bring the church "up to date" prior to the council. Conversely, the first phase cannot ignore its reciprocal dependence upon the second phase, which guides its proper implementation. Some aspects of contemporary historical Jesus research, for example, at times ignore the second phase.

Lonergan qualifies further that there is special reciprocal dependence between doctrines and history, and between foundations and dialectic (136). With respect to doctrines and history, doctrines can become antiquated or irrelevant if they ignore history. For example, currently deaconesses are prohibited by the official Roman Catholic Church, despite evidence from the early church – the Letters of Pliny the Younger, one of which refers to women deaconesses.[5] However, the reverse can happen when historians overstate their findings and try to supplant or overturn tradition. Some of the conclusions of the Jesus Seminar, for example, at times bypassed the other functional specialties (especially doctrines and systematics) and went straight to communications. To develop or better understand a doctrine, one must know the history of the doctrine as well as the content of the doctrine itself.

Dialectic and foundations have a reciprocal relationship as well. Dialectic brings to light differences that may signal a need for conversion. "Foundations objectifies conversion" (137). Whereas "dialectic brings to light the opposite poles in a conflict," foundations links them to a personal history. This in turn gives a gravitas to the differences brought to light within dialectic, and an existential call to change in foundations. But because the specialty foundations deals with personal histories, it cannot have the comprehensive aim that dialectic has.

In an easily overlooked difference between dialectic and foundations, Lonergan clarifies how decision is different between the two. Decision in dialectic is "partial" in the sense that it "tends to eliminate evidently foolish oppositions and so narrows down issues." However, it does not "go to the roots of all conflict," which ultimately lie in the human heart (134). In other words, decision in dialectic is to identify what differences are complementary, contradictory, or genetic, while the specialty foundations resolves particularly the contradictory differences that require psychological, intellectual, moral, or religious healing of the relevant block in development – this entails an existential decision on behalf of the researcher. The decision is essential in establishing the existential orientation from which doctrines will be derived.

The question emerges here whether the specialty foundations entails the conversion of the researcher? The answer would be affirmative, and a good example would be the work of the comparative theologian. In dialectic, the comparative theologian would set up a comparison and contrast between her home tradition and another. In so doing, she would identify various types of difference. Presumably, when she moves into foundations, she will attempt to resolve the differences she confronts in her own appropriation of the two traditions, or she may challenge her own tradition, or the alternative tradition she studies, to change. Consider how a Christian comparative theologian might confront the notion of reincarnation or the caste system in Hinduism: if she attempts to resolve differences she finds between Christianity and Hinduism, she will do so in foundations, and not in dialectic.[6]

Finally, Lonergan notes that an "indirect interdependence" exists between dialectic-foundations and history-doctrines insofar as each is implicitly dependent upon all eight specialties.

Conclusion

In the conclusion to this chapter, Lonergan summarizes what he is doing as conceiving theological method as *die Wendung zur Idee*. Borrowing the idea from Georg Simmel, Lonergan views his work as "the shift towards system" (137).[7] The editors of *CWL* 14 refer to it as a "displacement towards system" (134n4); but it is equally a movement towards a structured, ordered unity of diverse subject and field specializations.

It is the wisdom of order that Lonergan brings with his groundbreaking proposal: the mediated phase comprising four specialties that engage the past, and a mediating phase comprising four specialties oriented to the future. There is no need to choose between subject specialization and field specialization, since subject specialization pertains to the mediated phase and field specialization pertains to the mediating phase. Lonergan's proposal encapsulates the entire range of topics for scholarly theological inquiry.

Notes

Preface

1 See Lonergan, *A Second Collection*, vol. 13 of *Collected Works of Bernard Lonergan*, 48–59; henceforth cited parenthetically as *CWL* 13. I am grateful to Sr. McEnroy for introducing me to Lonergan's thought.
2 He initially made these comments at a Lonergan seminar at Boston College in 2020.
3 I have in mind here scholars like Dr. H. Daniel Monsour, perhaps the most knowledgeable and deepest thinker about Lonergan I have encountered in my career.

Introduction

1 Lonergan, "Functional Specialties: Breakthrough Page" (punctuation and emphasis added). The exact date, according to Robert Doran, is 5 February 1965 (personal communication, 1 June 2018). While functional specialization has yet to have significant impact, it is worth noting that the reorganization of the Graduate Centre at the Toronto School of Theology in 2014 did away with the former departments of biblical, pastoral, history, and systematics and decided to focus more on something close to what Lonergan understood as functional specialization. The administration did this, of course, unaware of Lonergan's theory.
2 Crowe, *Method in Theology*, 32.
3 See Rahner, "Towards a Fundamental Interpretation."
4 For the development of Lonergan's *Method in Theology* in the context of wisdom, see chap. 8, "Contemporary Method as Wisdom," in Allen, *Theological Method*, and also Dadosky, "Lonergan on Wisdom."
5 Holy See, *Pastoral Constitution*, 56.

134 Notes to pages 4–16

6 See, for example, Michael Polanyi's discussion of the "doctrine of doubt" in *Personal Knowledge*, 269–72.
7 Lonergan, *Method in Theology*, vol. 14 of *Collected Works of Bernard Lonergan*, 122; henceforth cited parenthetically by page number.
8 *Optatam totius*, Decree on Priestly Formation, Vatican II Documents, 28 October 1965, 14.
9 Rahner, *Foundations of Christian Faith*, 7.

1. Approaching Lonergan's *Method in Theology*: The Preface and Introduction

1 Lonergan, *Verbum*, vol. 2 of *Collected Works of Bernard Lonergan*; henceforth cited parenthetically as *CWL* 2.
2 See Lonergan, *Grace and Freedom*, vol. 1 of *Collected Works of Bernard Lonergan*; henceforth cited parenthetically as *CWL* 1.
3 Lonergan, *Insight*, vol. 3 of *Collected Works of Bernard Lonergan*; henceforth cited parenthetically as *CWL* 3.
4 Philip McShane, personal communication, 24 April 2018.
5 Doran, *Systematic Theology*, 53–60.
6 Lonergan, *Philosophical and Theological Papers*, vol. 6 of *Collected Works of Bernard Lonergan*, 115; henceforth cited parenthetically as *CWL* 6.
7 Doran, *Systematic Theology*, 56–7.
8 See also the editor's footnote 30 on p. 115 of *CWL* 6 for some further background on Lonergan's notion of mediation.
9 Lonergan, *Early Works 3*, vol. 24 of *Collected Works of Bernard Lonergan*, 142; henceforth cited parenthetically as *CWL* 24.
10 Lonergan, *A Second Collection*, vol. 13 of *Collected Works of Bernard Lonergan*, 55; henceforth cited parenthetically as *CWL* 13.
11 Doran, *Systematic Theology*, 57.
12 See Crowe, "The Church as Learner."
13 Doran, *Systematic Theology*, 58.
14 Doran, 59.
15 I will give one example of many from Vatican II. *Gaudium et spes*, 44, states: "Just as it is in the world's interest to acknowledge the Church as a historical reality … the Church herself knows how richly she has profited by the history and development of humanity."
16 I have worked out the groundwork and development of Lonergan's notion of mutual self-mediation and friendship. See Dadosky, "Has Vatican II Been Hermeneutered?"
17 Doran, *Systematic Theology*, 59.
18 Seeing as Constantine did not implement forced conversions, it might be better to refer to it as the end of the era of Charlemagne and the later

colonial expansions. One could speculate that without the Constantinian Peace (314 AD), Christianity would not have survived subsequent generations.
19 See Bosch, *Transforming Mission*.
20 An initial version of this essay was conceived as the first chapter of *Method in Theology*. That original draft in edited form is available as appendix 1 of *Method* (*CWL* 14).
21 Harris, *History of Theories of Culture*, 10–11.
22 See, for example, the report of the Truth and Reconciliation Commission in Canada: https://nctr.ca/records/reports/#trc-reports.
23 O'Hara, *Curiosity*, 427.
24 Lonergan initially had interest in a philosophy of history but was told at the last minute that he would do a doctorate in theology and not philosophy. It is clear from his early papers that the notion of a philosophy of history was with him from the beginning. See Lonergan, *Archival Material*, vol. 25 of *Collected Works of Bernard Lonergan*; henceforth cited parenthetically as *CWL* 25. See also Lonergan, "Transition from a Classicist Worldview," in *CWL* 13, 3–10; and Crowe, "All My Work."
25 Quoted in O'Hara, *Curiosity at the Center*, 426.
26 See, for example, Doran, *Theology and the Dialectics of History*, 421–39; Curnow, *Preferential Option*; and Whelan, *A Discerning Church*.

2. Method

1 Although more commonly Lonergan refers to the first level as "experience," he also refers to it as "presentations," the data presented to the five senses or the imagination. This duality in terminology has not been picked up on by students of Lonergan, but is worth mentioning here (see *CWL* 3, 298).
2 Lonergan, *Ontological and Psychological Constitution of Christ*, vol. 7 of *Collected Works of Bernard Lonergan*, 161; henceforth cited parenthetically as *CWL* 7.
3 Binswanger, "Dream and Existence."
4 In one of his later essays, "Towards a Post-Hegelian Philosophy of Religion," Lonergan is very explicit about how each level of intentional consciousness opens up incrementally into fuller realization of self-transcendence – the level of decision is the fullest expression in two aspects: (1) when one takes possession of one's freedom in a self-constitutive way, and (2) when one commits to be in love with one's family, friends, community, and God (*CWL* 16, 200–1).
5 In one of his lectures on method, Lonergan adds "deciding to be authentic" ("Lectures on Method in Theology" [1970], 3). This suggests that, as self-constituting people, we are responsible for our own authenticity.

6 Lonergan, *The Triune God*, vol. 12 of *Collected Works of Bernard Lonergan*, 179; henceforth cited parenthetically as *CWL* 12.
7 While Lonergan does not use the sphericity of the moon example in *Method*, it appears in other places. For example, see *CWL* 13, 176.
8 On p. 16 of the text, in the example of elementary and compound knowing, Lonergan distinguishes conception from understanding. Conception is an elementary component in the group of operations that form the second level of understanding (inquiring, insight, hypothesis, conception, etc.). In this example, Lonergan likely means by "understanding" the insight into the unity of the data or the relations among the data.
9 This fourfold distinction is fairly exhaustive of Lonergan's understanding of bias. I will return to it in more detail in the discussion of bias.
10 In *CWL* 7, Lonergan states:

> A subject is rendered conscious through its operations in accordance with the perfection of the operations themselves. Thus, through sensitive operations one is rendered empirically conscious; through inquiry, understanding, and conception one becomes intellectually conscious; through reflection, weighing the evidence, and judgment one becomes rationally conscious; and through seeking intelligible good, deliberating about it, and choosing it one becomes morally conscious. Moreover, since there is an order among these levels of consciousness, in which the higher presupposes the lower, it is possible to have empirical consciousness without intellectual, intellectual without rational, and rational without moral; but you cannot have moral consciousness without rational, rational without intellectual, or intellectual without empirical. This, however, describes the natural order which, in a way, is reversible, since God by the infusion of supernatural graces can and usually does affect the will more than the intellect and the intellect more than the senses. (187)

11 Dadosky, *Eclipse and Recovery*.
12 Cited in *Method in Theology*, 16–17n10; Lonergan, Q&A Session from Institute on Method in Theology, Dublin, 1971.
13 Cited in Dadosky, *Eclipse and Recovery*, 52; Lonergan, Q&A Session from Method in Theology Lectures, Regis College, 28–9.
14 See Dadosky, *Eclipse and Recovery*.
15 Lonergan uses the term in a Scholastic sense, in contrast to the "categorial (or predicamental)" sense (17n11). With respect to epistemology, Lonergan is *not* a Kantian or a neo-Kantian. This is not to say that Lonergan's philosophy does not have *a priori* components that are "transcendental" in the Kantian sense, at least in a qualified manner. Giovani Sala distinguishes Lonergan's epistemology from that of Kant, suggesting

that the former provides a corrective to the latter. Sala states: "The merit of *Insight* [Lonergan's philosophical position] lies in its having advanced the transcendental analysis begun in the KRV [*Critique of Pure Reason*], bringing to light the conditions for the possibility of objective knowledge. This has resulted in a threefold clarification: (1) of the a priori as the conscious-subjective dimension of knowledge, (2) of knowledge as an empirical, intelligent, and rational structure, and (3) of reality as intrinsically intelligible" (*Lonergan and Kant*, 32).

16 The editors point out that Lonergan uses the term "generalized empirical method" (GEM) for transcendental method (TM) in his earlier and later writings, but not in *Method in Theology*. In the same note, Lonergan distinguishes his notion of transcendental method from Otto Muck's use of the term (17n11).

17 In earlier writings, Lonergan had not yet distinguished the transcendental precepts fully from the functional specialties, and so he speaks of five precepts that are a combination of both precepts and functional specialties. See chap. 2 of *CWL* 6 and chap. 4 of Lonergan, *Early Works 1*, vol. 22 of *Collected Works of Bernard Lonergan*; henceforth cited parenthetically as *CWL* 22.

18 Johnson with Ruhl, *Balancing Heaven and Earth*, 141–2.

19 One must keep in mind that Lonergan often presumes originating and creative insights in his examples in order to make the point. In reality, many insights come to us through ordinary meaning (we recognize a traffic signal, for example). There is here room for Wittgenstein's insight into ordinary language to complement Lonergan's work. The notion of originating insights would provide a corrective to Wittgenstein's famous word-game, insofar as the latter's philosophy cannot account for immanently generated creative insights, leaps in our intelligibility and human knowledge. Wittgenstein's "insight" into word-games is not itself the product of a word-game, but rather of an immanently generated insight. This point will come up again in chap. 3 on meaning, but the reader may want to consult Robert Doran's articles on the topic: "Reception and Elemental Meaning" and "Insight and Language."

20 Lavine, *Socrates to Sartre*, 201–2.

21 For example, see Lonergan's example of Tertullian and Origen in his essay "The Origins of Christian Realism," *CWL* 13, 206–12.

22 Dadosky, *Eclipse and Recovery*, 20.

23 Lonergan, "Lectures on Method in Theology" (1970), 1.

3. Apprehending and Doing the Good

1 However, as we will see, the judgment of value is clearly distinguished in chap. 20 of *Insight* in his discussion of belief.

2 See Lonergan, *Phenomenology and Logic*, vol. 18 of *Collected Works of Bernard Lonergan*; henceforth cited parenthetically as *CWL 18*.
3 Robert Doran, personal communication.
4 Lonergan, *Understanding and Being*, vol. 5 of *Collected Works of Bernard Lonergan*; henceforth cited parenthetically as *CWL 5*.
5 Lonergan, *Topics in Education*, vol. 10 of *Collected Works of Bernard Lonergan*; henceforth cited parenthetically as *CWL 10*.
6 See *CWL 10*, chap. 8. The editors mention that Lonergan specifically read Piaget for these lectures on education (xiii). "Insofar, then, as Piaget's notion of differentiation or separability of assimilation and adjustment is correct, there is a validity to the notion of general education that studies language, art, literature, history and philosophy rather than the human sciences, and mathematics rather than the natural sciences" (206).
7 Newman, *Grammar of Assent*, 83.
8 Actually, one could add a third way, as certain Buddhist lineages do, that of "neutral" responses to value; but I suspect this would be seen as either a non-response or an aggregable one insofar what is responded to as neutral would not be disagreeable.
9 He repeats this almost verbatim later in the chapter: "the ontic value of a person or the qualitative value of beauty, of understanding, of truth, of noble deeds, of virtuous acts, of great achievements" (39).
10 In chap. 1, he makes a similar association: "moral pursuit of goodness [decision], a philosophic pursuit of truth [judgment], a scientific pursuit of understanding [understanding], an artistic pursuit of beauty [experience?]" (16). See the reference to archival data in footnote 10 on the same page. "[Beauty is] a total response of the person to an object."
11 See the discussion in chap. 2.
12 In *The Eclipse and Recovery of Beauty*, I suggest that *intelligibility* pertains to the transcendental *unity*. See chap. 6, 148.
13 Arthur Danto *attempts* to preserve the relevance of beauty in art and aesthetics discourse. See his *Abuse of Beauty*. See also chap. 8 in my *Eclipse and Recovery*.
14 See Bajzek, "Alterity, Similarity, and Dialectic"; Kanaris and Doorley, *In Deference to the Other*; Saracino, *On Being Human*; Blackwood, *Hope Does Not Disappoint*; and Kaplan, *René Girard, Unlikely Apologist*.
15 Patrick Byrne has completed perhaps the most extensive study of the background on Lonergan's use of the scale of preference. See chap. 9 of his *Ethics of Discernment*. One could quibble that his book could have been more accurately titled *Ethics as Discernment*, since, for Lonergan, much ethical deliberation *is* discernment.
16 Byrne suggests the following vital values: "nutrition, growth, development, flourishing and fertility" (*Ethics of Discernment*, 261). The

first, nutrition, would probably fall under health as a vital value. Growth and development would not be vital values per se but rather the fruits of choosing vital values, all things being equal. Growth and development reflect the proper unfolding of underlying laws of genetic development of which the individual may have little control or ability to choose. Byrne is likely correct that propagation (he also uses the term "procreation") is a vital value, but it would be one conditioned by cultural, personal, and religious values.

17 Byrne includes among these values "cooperative effort, order, dependability, efficiency, justice-as-fairness, and social tranquility" (*Ethics of Discernment*, 262).
18 See *CWL* 10, 34–6.
19 In chap. 7 of *Insight* (242–4), Lonergan identifies a basic dialectic of community that negotiates a linked but opposed principle between spontaneous intersubjectivity and practical intelligence.
20 Curiously, Byrne (*Ethics of Discernment*, 262–3) does not identify the key role of art, aesthetics, and literature in cultural value, especially in promoting development within a community. Nevertheless, these topics are important to Lonergan's notion of cultural value. See Dadosky, *Eclipse*, 160, 172–3.
21 Much more could be said on Lonergan's notion of culture, his shift from a classicist to an empirical one, and his intriguing comments on the philosophy of culture. See the discussion in chap. 1.
22 On these three in the ethical sphere, see Price, *The Narrow Pass*, 171–80.
23 Doran, *Theology and the Dialectics of History*, 95.
24 See Ogbonnaya, *Lonergan, Social Transformation*.
25 See the quotation of Lonergan's from Michael Vertin's interview with him in Vertin, "Judgments of Value," 235n46.
26 Scheler, *Ressentiment*.
27 Apropos this discussion, certain lineages in Buddhism focus on the *kleshas*, strong affectivity, *shenpa*, the energy underneath the affectivity, and the *shaky tenderness* beneath the *shenpa*. Special breathing techniques allow one to address such dramatic emotional energy. See Chödron, *Living Beautifully*.
28 See Doran, *TDH*, chap. 6, for his fullest account of *psychic* conversion, a development Lonergan accepted. I have argued previously and continue to maintain that any healing of a subject's block in psychological development should be more broadly referred to as *psychological conversion*. Psychic conversion has a role to play in that process.
29 "Autonomous spiritual procession" is a phrase invoked by Robert Doran to refer to intellectual emanations wherein act proceeds from act. See his *Missions and Processions*, 183–7.

140 Notes to pages 56–63

30 See chap. 7 of Dadosky, *Eclipse and Recovery*.
31 See Lonergan, *Archival Material*, vol. 25 of *Collected Works of Bernard Lonergan*; henceforth cited parenthetically as *CWL 25*.
32 de Finance, *Essai sur l'agir humain*.
33 Ignatius of Loyola, *Spiritual Exercises*, no. 95.
34 It is interesting to ponder whether there is also a false desolation, whereby we may fear making the right decision, or feel ill at ease having made it, or whereby consolation in having made it is not immediate.
35 Some of the exposition in this section has been adapted from Dadosky, "God's Eternal Yes!"
36 See Doran, "General Editors' Preface," *CWL 16*, xii–xiii.
37 Doran, *Missions and Processions*, 161.
38 See *CWL 18*.
39 Fleming, *Draw Me*, 138. Doran, concerning the first time of election, states that conscious representation of "*gratia gratum faciens*" and its word of value judgment are so dominant that the loving decisions and actions flow spontaneously forth from them in a way that admits no doubt as to where they come from or whose life is being reflected in them: "I live, now not I, but Christ lives in me." This corresponds to Lonergan's modification of an Augustinian maxim, "*Ama Deum et fac quod vis*, Love God and do what you will." In these instances, the apprehension of values in loving affectivity stands to judgments of value, not as direct insight, which may be right or wrong, but rather as reflective insights, grasping the fulfilment of conditions, stand to judgments of fact. Whereas in the second time the apprehension of values in feelings is an apprehension of possible values, in the first time there are no further questions, and one knows that this is the case. (*Missions and Processions*, 161)
40 Fleming, *Spiritual Exercises*, 138.
41 Fleming, 138.
42 Doran, "Ignatian Themes," 94–5.
43 See *CWL 3*, 632–9, 650–6.
44 An affective grasp of value would also be rational; but the apprehension of value occurs in one's feelings rather than with one's intellect.
45 Byrne's *Ethics of Discernment* does not account for the third time of election or what I have called rational, indirectly affective grasps of value. If he is going to bring in Ignatian discernment, then he would have to account for the third time of election.
46 Some of the exposition in this section has been adapted from chap. 7 of Dadosky, *Eclipse and Recovery*.
47 Crowe, "Complacency and Concern."
48 Crowe, 83.
49 Crowe, 90.

50 Vertin, "Judgments of Value," 228.
51 Vertin, 241n58.

4. Different Types of Meaning

1 See Langer, *Feeling and Form*, 59–60n5.
2 See Alexander, *Phenomenon of Life*.
3 See Dadosky, *Eclipse and Recovery*, 182–94.
4 See chap. 6 of Doran's *TDH*.
5 Dadosky, "Sacred Symbols."
6 See Doran, *Systematic Theology*, 16.
7 In his text, Lonergan distinguishes between *active meanings* and *instrumental acts* of meanings. Here, I put them together because each correlates with the fourth level, decision.
8 See chap. 19 of Lonergan's *Insight* (*CWL* 3) for his argument for God's existence.
9 Some of the exposition in this section has been adapted from Dadosky, "Is There a Fourth Stage."
10 Distinguishing and grouping *decision* with *commitment* is not Lonergan's explicit wording. It comes from my own thinking about the fifth level as distinct from the fourth level, by distinguishing decision (fourth level) from commitment (fifth level). The latter effects and prolongs the state of being in love. See, for example, *CWL* 14, 109.
11 I prescind here from the question of whether the stages of meaning can be applied outside of the Western context. Certainly, Lonergan's emphasis on a shift from a classicist or normative notion of culture to an empirical one supports such a possibility. Cyril Orji has attempted to identify the stages of meaning in the context of African theology. See his "Are There Stages of Meaning?" Moreover, it may very well be that the Asian religions have a more differentiated notion of interiority, given the influence of Hinduism and Buddhism over the centuries. This may be one of the reasons why pioneers of inter-religious dialogue such as Thomas Merton saw value in the Eastern religions in their desire to understand monastic contemplation more fully. Unfortunately, this interesting question is beyond the scope of this book.
12 Lonergan, draft chapter 5, "Meaning," 40.
13 See Dadosky, "Eliade and Girard on Myth."
14 Copleston, *Greece and Rome*, 257.
15 This application of the critical and systematic exigencies to the stages of meaning concurs with the view of Robert Doran (*TDH*, 582).
16 Polanyi, *Personal Knowledge*, 269–72.
17 See Lévy-Bruhl, *How Natives Think*. While the idea that "Westerners" and Indigenous peoples think differently is not necessarily problematic, Lévy-

Bruhl was criticized for this theory, and he later retracted it; for a critical summary of Lévy-Bruhl's work, see Evans-Pritchard, *Theories of Primitive Religion*, 78–99. More recently, however, the Harvard anthropologist Stanley J. Tambiah has argued for a qualified recovery of some of Lévy-Bruhl's insights: see Tambiah, *Magic, Science*, 84–110. The tendency to posit fundamental differences between Western European and Aboriginal/Indigenous ways of thinking is often associated with Lévy-Bruhl's strongly criticized theory of "primitive mentality," and so there is a temptation to dismiss any theory exhibiting some form of this tendency. However, more recent scholarship has begun to view Lévy-Bruhl's theory in a renewed light. Tambiah writes: "I am tempted to say that what Lévy-Bruhl was striving to characterize as the process of participation and mystical orientation was concordant with the process of presentational and iconic coding as proposed by Langer, Freud, and Bateson" (*Magic, Science*, 95). Moreover, the notion of *differentiations of consciousness* provides a way of understanding the different styles of thinking without positing a preference for a particular style.

18 Eriksen and Nielsen, *History of Anthropology*, 50.
19 Crowe, *Old Things and New*, chap. 2.
20 Lonergan did not explicitly mention *intellectualist bias*; the idea has been developed by this author, Robert M. Doran, and Dennis Doyle, independently of one another.
21 In his article "Interpreting Lonergan's View of Method in 1954," Patrick Brown rightly stated that I was not entirely correct when I asserted in my original essay, "Is There a Fourth Stage of Meaning?," that Lonergan never mentioned a fourth stage of meaning. In fact, Lonergan did use the phrase "fourth stage," as Brown points out, and I corrected myself in a subsequent publication, which Brown does not cite. See Dadosky, "Midwiving the Fourth Stage," 71–92. See also Lonergan, draft chapter 5, "Meaning."
22 Lonergan was influenced by Whitson's text and speaks of it in his essay "Prolegomena to the Study of the Emerging Religious Consciousness of our Time," in *CWL* 16, 63–4.
23 Fowler, *Stages of Faith*, esp. chap. 6.
24 See Dadosky, "Is There a Fourth Stage," 773–5.
25 Hefling, "Lonergan's *Cur Deus Homo*," 156.
26 Frederick Crowe uses "the level of the times" as an extended analogy in his introduction to Lonergan's thought: see his *Lonergan*, esp. 58.
27 Lonergan, letter to Thomas O'Malley, 2; see Rixon, "O'Malley," 77–86.
28 See Dadosky and Krokus, "What Are Comparative Theologians Doing?"
29 Lonergan, draft chapter 5, "Meaning."
30 Lonergan, 42b.
31 See esp. chaps. 1, 3, 5, and 9 ("Homer's View of Man," "The Rise of the Individual in the Early Greek Lyric," "Myth and Reality in Greek Tragedy," and "From Myth to Logic: The Role of Comparison," respectively).

32 In distinguishing between *minor* and *major* I am following Lonergan. See *CWL* 14, 118.
33 See chap. 3, note 12.

5. Lonergan's Notion of "Genuine" Religion

1 *CWL* 3.
2 *CWL* 11 and 12.
3 Dadosky, *Eclipse and Recovery*, 161.
4 The introductory paragraphs are taken from Dadosky, "Further Along the Fourth Stage," 72. Parts of the present chapter have been adapted from this article.
5 Quoting from editor's note, *CWL* 14, 101n8. See also Lonergan, "Lectures on Method in Theology" (1971), 5–8.
6 See especially his work on operative grace in *CWL* 1.
7 In fact, Albert Camus died in a tragic car accident, which makes one wonder how he answered the question for himself – insofar as recklessness can go together with a sense of meaninglessness or arbitrariness concerning one's freedom.
8 Price, *The Narrow Pass*, 161–70.
9 von Balthasar, "Revelation and the Beautiful," 96.
10 Dadosky, *Eclipse and Recovery*, 86–99.
11 Lonergan omits patience from the list!
12 Crowe, "Universalist Notion of Religion," 159.
13 This section and the next have been adapted from Dadosky, "Further Along the Fourth Stage," 72–6.
14 The major religions Lonergan lists are Christianity, Judaism, Islam, Zoroastrian Mazdaism, Hinduism, Buddhism, and Taoism (105). Crowe points out that Lonergan, likely because of his theological commitments, which included a liberal belief in God's generosity in distributing grace, was open to expanding his list to include Indigenous religions. See Crowe, "Universalist Notion of Religion," 161. See also Lonergan, "Faith and Beliefs," in *Philosophical and Theological Papers*, vol. 17 of *Collected Works of Bernard Lonergan*, 42 (henceforth cited parenthetically as *CWL* 17), and Lonergan, "A Post-Hegelian Philosophy of Religion," in *CWL* 16, 194–213.
15 See Heiler, "History of Religions." Heiler's actual wording is as follows: (1) "The first is the reality of the transcendent, the holy, the divine, the Other"; (2) "this transcendent reality is immanent in human hearts"; (3) "this reality is … the highest good, the highest truth, righteousness, goodness, and beauty"; (4) "this reality of the Divine is ultimate love which reveals itself to [human beings] and in [human beings]"; (5) "the way of [humanity] to God is universally the way of sacrifice"; (6) "all high

religions teach not only the way to God, but always and at the same time the way to the neighbor as well"; and (7) "love is the most superior way to God" [as "ultimate goal"]..
16 Note Lonergan does not follow Heiler here as he leaves out supreme beauty!
17 For example, *CWL* 16, 69; also Crowe states: "The appeal to the divine salvific will is straightforward Roman Catholic doctrine" ("Universalist Notion of Religion," 160). See also p. 159 of the same article for references to universal salvation.
18 For example, see Nasr, foreword to *Divine Love*, xi.
19 Dadosky, "Naming the Demon."
20 I am interpreting Massignon here: he does not use the language of the two foci. See Krokus, *Theology of Louis Massignon*, 191–2.
21 See Raab, "Encountering Others."
22 See Panikkar, *The Intrareligious Dialogue*.
23 "Nothing is loved unless it is first known."
24 I have argued elsewhere that romantic, committed love between two persons implies a privileged access to each other's central form and acts. See Dadosky, *Eclipse and Recovery*, 199–200.
25 A reference in the editorial notes cites the Regis College 1969 Lectures on Method on this point: "The person that is in love doesn't try to explain it or account for it; he just acts" (118n26).
26 This section has been adapted with some editorial changes from Dadosky, "Further Along the Fourth Stage," 77–9.
27 Pope Francis, foreword to Apostolic Constitution *Veritatis gaudium*, no. 3; emphasis added.
28 Lonergan never explained what he means by "personal value," but one could safely presume he means committed love, friendships, and vocation (broadly understood).
29 On the fifth level, see Blackwood, *Hope Does Not Disappoint*.
30 Lonergan, "Religious Commitment," 56–7.
31 See the final chapter, "Final Integration – Toward a 'Monastic Therapy,'" in Merton, *Contemplation*.
32 Merton, *Contemplation*, 212.

6. Ordered Wisdom: The Eight Functional Specialties

1 While not a conversion that Lonergan proposed, psychological conversion heals the blocks in development caused by dramatic bias.
2 See Doran, *TDH*, chap. 6.
3 Lonergan does not mention dialogue with other Christian denominations; such dialogue would likely be the prerogative of foundations, since all Christians share a belief in Jesus Christ.

4 Lonergan's nomenclature in this section is unfortunate when he speaks of "systematics fixing the kernel of the message to be communicated in many different ways" (135). One must not associate this with the kernel and husk that was popularized through the legacy of Adolf von Harnack, since for Lonergan gospel and culture are inextricably intertwined, and are constitutive of one another.
5 See Letter 10.96, bk. 10, in "Pliny the Younger: Letters," *Attalus*, accessed 30 October 2023, https://www.attalus.org/info/pliny.html.
6 See Dadosky and Krokus, "What Are Comparative Theologians Doing?"
7 See Simmel, "Die Wendung zur Idee."

Bibliography

Alexander, Christopher. *The Phenomenon of Life*. Vol. 1 of *The Nature of Order: An Essay on the Art of Building and the Nature of the Universe*. Berkeley, CA: Center for Environmental Structure, 2002.

Allen, Paul L. *Theological Method: A Guide for the Perplexed*. London: T&T Clark, 2012.

Bajzek, Brian. "Alterity, Similarity, and Dialectic: Methodological Reflections on the Turn to the Other." *International Philosophical Quarterly* 57, no. 3 (September 2017): 249–66. https://doi.org/10.5840/ipq20176788.

Binswanger, Ludwig. "Dream and Existence." In *Being-in-the-World: Selected Papers of Ludwig Binswanger*, translated by Jacob Needleman, 222–48. New York: Harper Torchbooks, 1963. Originally published as *Le rêve et l'existence* (Paris: Desclée, 1954).

Blackwood, Jeremy W. *And Hope Does Not Disappoint: Love, Grace, and Subjectivity in the Work of Bernard J. F. Lonergan, S.J.* Milwaukee: Marquette University Press, 2017.

Bosch, David J. *Transforming Mission: Paradigm Shifts in Theology of Mission*. Twentieth anniversary edition. Maryknoll, NY: Orbis Books, 2011.

Byrne, Patrick. *Ethics of Discernment*. Toronto: University of Toronto Press, 2016.

Chödron, Pema. *Living Beautifully: With Uncertainty and Change*. Boston: Shambhala, 2012.

Copleston, Frederick. *Greece and Rome*. Vol. 1 of *History of Philosophy*. New York: Doubleday, 1993.

Crowe, Frederick E. "All My Work Has Been Introducing History into Catholic Theology." In *Developing the Lonergan Legacy: Historical, Theoretical, and Existential Themes*, edited by Michael Vertin, 78–110. Toronto: University of Toronto Press, 2004.

– "The Church as Learner: Two Crises, One Kairos." In *Appropriating the Lonergan Idea*, edited by Michael Vertin, 371–84. Toronto: University of Toronto Press, 2006.

- "Complacency and Concern in the Thought of St. Thomas Aquinas." In *Three Thomist Studies*, 73–187. Boston: Boston College, 2000.
- *Lonergan*. Outstanding Christian Thinkers. New York: Geoffrey Chapman, 1992.
- "Lonergan's Universalist Notion of Religion." *Method: Journal of Lonergan Studies* 12 (Fall 1994): 147–79. https://doi.org/10.5840/method19941224.
- *Method in Theology: An Organon for Our Time*. The 1980 Père Marquette Theology Lecture. Milwaukee, WI: Marquette University Press, 1980.
- *Old Things and New: A Strategy for Education*. New York: Scholars Press, 1985.

Curnow, Rohan. *The Preferential Option for the Poor: A Short History and a Reading Based on the Thought of Bernard Lonergan*. Milwaukee, WI: Marquette University Press, 2014.

Dadosky, John D. *The Eclipse and Recovery of Beauty: A Lonergan Approach*. Toronto: University of Toronto Press, 2014.
- "Eliade and Girard on Myth." In *Mircea Eliade: Myth, Religion, and History*, edited by Nicolae Babuts, 64–77. Piscataway, NJ: Transaction, 2014.
- "Further Along the Fourth Stage of Meaning: Lonergan, Alterity and Genuine Religion." *Irish Theological Quarterly* 85, no. 1 (February 2020): 64–79. https://doi.org/10.1177/0021140019889214.
- "'God's Eternal Yes!': An Exposition and Development of Lonergan's Psychological Analogy of the Trinity." *Irish Theological Quarterly* 81, no. 4 (November 2016): 397–419. https://doi.org/10.1177/0021140016659714.
- "Has Vatican II been Hermeneutered?: Recovering and Developing Its Theological Achievements Following Rahner and Lonergan." *Irish Theological Quarterly* 79, no. 4 (November 2014): 327–49. https://doi.org/10.1177/0021140014541372.
- "Is There a Fourth Stage of Meaning?" *Heythrop Journal* 51, no. 5 (September 2010): 768–80. https://doi.org/10.1111/j.1468-2265.2009.00518.x.
- "Lonergan on Wisdom." *Irish Theological Quarterly* 79, no. 1 (February 2014): 45–67. https://doi.org/10.1177/0021140013509437.
- "Midwiving the Fourth Stage of Meaning: Lonergan and Doran." In *Meaning and History in Systematic Theology: Essays in Honor of Robert M. Doran, SJ*, edited by John Dadosky, 71–92. Milwaukee, WI: Marquette University Press, 2009.
- "'Naming the Demon': The 'Structure' of Evil in Lonergan and Girard." *Irish Theological Quarterly* 75, no. 4 (November 2010): 355–72. https://doi.org/10.1177/0021140010377736.
- "Sacred Symbols as Explanatory: Geertz, Eliade and Lonergan." *Fu Jen International Religious Studies* 4, no. 1 (Summer 2010): 137–58. https://doi.org/10.29448/FJIRS.201006.0007.

Dadosky, John D., and Christian Krokus. "What Are Comparative Theologians Doing When They Are Doing Comparative Theology?: A Lonerganian

Perspective with Examples from the Engagement with Islam." *Studies in Interreligious Dialogue* 32, no. 1 (2022): 67–93. https://doi.org/10.2143/SID.32.1.3290944.

Danto, Arthur. *The Abuse of Beauty: Aesthetics and the Concept of Art*. Peru, IL: Open Court, 2003.

Dawson, Christopher. *The Age of the Gods: A Study in the Origins of Culture in Prehistoric Europe and the Ancient East*. London: Sheed and Ward, 1928.

Doran, Robert M. "Ignatian Themes in the Thought of Bernard Lonergan: Revisiting a Theme That Deserves Further Reflection." *Journal of the Lonergan Workshop* 19 (2006): 83–106.

– "Insight and Language: Steps towards the Resolution of a Problem." *Divyadaan* 15, no. 3 (2004): 405–26.

– *Missions and Processions*. Vol. 1 of *The Trinity in History: A Theology of the Divine Missions*. Toronto: University of Toronto Press, 2019.

– "Reception and Elemental Meaning: An Expansion of the Notion of Psychic Conversion." *Toronto Journal of Theology* 20, no. 2 (September 2004): 133–57. https://doi.org/10.3138/tjt.20.2.133.

– *Theology and the Dialectics of History*. Toronto: University of Toronto Press, 1990.

– *What Is Systematic Theology?* Toronto: University of Toronto Press, 2005.

Eriksen, Thomas H., and Finn S. Nielsen. *A History of Anthropology*. London: Pluto, 2001.

Evans-Pritchard, E.E. *Theories of Primitive Religion*. Oxford: Clarendon, 1965.

de Finance, Joseph. *Essai sur l'agir humain*. Rome: Presses de l'Université Grégorienne, 1962.

Fleming, David L. *Draw Me into Your Friendship: A Literal Translation and a Contemporary Reading of the Spiritual Exercises*. St. Louis, MI: Institute of Jesuit Sources, 1996.

Fowler, James. *Stages of Faith: The Psychology of Human Development and the Quest for Meaning*. San Francisco: HarperCollins, 1981.

Francis, Pope. Apostolic Constitution *Veritatis gaudium* on Ecclesiastical Universities and Faculties. Rome, 8 December 2017.

Harris, Marvin. *A History of Theories of Culture*. New York: Thomas Y. Crowell, 1968.

Hefling, Charles. "Lonergan's *Cur Deus Homo*: Revisiting the 'Law of the Cross.'" In *Meaning and History in Systematic Theology: Essays in Honor of Robert M. Doran, SJ*, edited by John Dadosky, 145–66. Milwaukee, WI: Marquette University Press, 2009.

Heiler, Friedrich. "The History of Religions as a Preparation for the Co-operation of Religions." In *The History of Religions: Essays in Methodology*, edited by Mircea Eliade and Joseph M. Kitagawa, 142–60. Chicago: University of Chicago Press, 1962. Prepared for the Religion Online by Ted and Winnie Brock, https://www.religion-online.org/book-chapter/the-history-of

-religions-as-a-preparation-for-the-co-operation-of-religions-by-friedrich
-heiler/.
The Holy See. *Optatam totius*, Decree on Priestly Formation. Vatican II
Documents. 28 October 1965. https://www.vatican.va/archive/hist
_councils/ii_vatican_council/documents/vat-ii_decree_19651028_optatam
-totius_en.html.
The Holy See. *Pastoral Constitution on the Church in the Modern World:
Gaudium et Spes.* Vatican II Documents. 7 December 1965. https://www
.vatican.va/archive/hist_councils/ii_vatican_council/documents/vat-ii
_const_19651207_gaudium-et-spes_en.html.
Johnson, Robert A., with Jerry M. Ruhl. *Balancing Heaven and Earth.* New York:
HarperCollins, 2009.
Kanaris, Jim, and Mark J. Doorley, eds. *In Deference to the Other: Lonergan and
Contemporary Continental Thought.* Albany, NY: State University of New York
Press, 2004.
Kaplan, Grant. *René Girard, Unlikely Apologist: Mimetic Theory and Fundamental
Theology.* Notre Dame, IN: University of Notre Dame Press, 2016.
Krokus, Christian. *The Theology of Louis Massignon: Islam, Christ, and the Church.*
Washington, DC: Catholic University of America Press, 2017.
Langer, Susanne. *Feeling and Form: A Theory of Art.* New York: Charles
Scribner's Sons, 1953.
Lavine, T.Z. *Socrates to Sartre: The Philosophic Quest.* New York: Bantam Books, 1984.
Lévy-Bruhl, Lucien. *How Natives Think.* Translated by Lilian A. Claire.
Princeton, NY: Princeton University Press, 1985.
Lonergan, Bernard. *Archival Material: Early Papers on History.* Edited by
Robert M. Doran and John D. Dadosky. Vol. 25 of *Collected Works of Bernard
Lonergan.* Toronto: University of Toronto Press, 2019.
– Draft chapter 5, "Meaning," of *Method in Theology.* Bernard Lonergan
Archive, #73200DTE060. https://bernardlonergan.com/archive
/73200dte060/.
– *Early Works on Theological Method 1.* Edited by Robert M. Doran and Robert
C. Croken. Vol. 22 of *Collected Works of Bernard Lonergan.* Toronto: University
of Toronto Press, 2010.
– *Early Works on Theological Method 3.* Edited by Robert M. Doran and H.
Daniel Monsour. Translated by Michael G. Shields. Vol. 24 of *Collected Works
of Bernard Lonergan.* Toronto: University of Toronto Press, 2013.
– "Faith and Beliefs." In *Philosophical and Theological Papers: 1965–1980*, 30–48.
Edited by Robert C. Croken and Robert M. Doran. Vol. 17 of *Collected Works
of Bernard Lonergan.* Toronto: University of Toronto Press, 2004.
– "Functional Specialties: Breakthrough Page." Bernard Lonergan Archive,
#47200D0E060 / A472 V71. https://bernardlonergan.com/archive
/47200d0e060/.

– *Grace and Freedom: Operative Grace in the Thought of St. Thomas Aquinas*. Edited by Frederick E. Crowe and Robert M. Doran. Vol. 1 of *Collected Works of Bernard Lonergan*. Toronto: University of Toronto Press, 2000.
– *Insight: A Study of Human Understanding*. Edited by Frederick E. Crowe and Robert M. Doran. Vol. 3 of *Collected Works of Bernard Lonergan*. Toronto: University of Toronto Press, 1992.
– "Lectures on Method in Theology," 14 June 1970, Boston College. Bernard Lonergan Archive, #592BCDTE070, p. 1. https://bernardlonergan.com/archive/592bcdte070/.
– "Lectures on Method in Theology," 4 August 1971, Dublin Institute. Bernard Lonergan Archive, #642B0DTE070. https://bernardlonergan.com/archive/642b0dte070/.
– Letter to Thomas O'Malley, 8 November 1978. Bernard Lonergan Archive, #32090DTE070 / A3209. https://www.bernardlonergan.com/archive/32090dte070/.
– "Bernard Lonergan to Thomas O'Malley, November 8, 1978." Edited by Gordon Rixon. *Method: Journal of Lonergan Studies* 20, no. 1 (Spring 2002): 77–86. https://doi.org/10.5840/method20022019.
– *Method in Theology*. Edited by Robert M. Doran and John D. Dadosky. Vol. 14 of *Collected Works of Bernard Lonergan*. Toronto: University of Toronto Press, 2017.
– *The Ontological and Psychological Constitution of Christ*. Translated by Michael G. Shields. Vol. 7 of *Collected Works of Bernard Lonergan*. Toronto: University of Toronto Press, 2002.
– *Phenomenology and Logic: The Boston College Lectures on Mathematical Logic and Existentialism*. Edited by Philip J. McShane. Vol. 18 of *Collected Works of Bernard Lonergan*. Toronto: University of Toronto Press, 2001.
– *Philosophical and Theological Papers, 1958–1964*. Edited by Robert C. Croken, Frederick E. Crowe, and Robert M. Doran. Vol. 6 of *Collected Works of Bernard Lonergan*. Toronto: University of Toronto Press, 1996.
– Q&A Session from Institute on Method in Theology, Dublin, 1971. Bernard Lonergan Archive, A185/#18510DTE070. https://bernardlonergan.com/archive/18510dte070/.
– Q&A Session from Method in Theology Lectures, Regis College, 17 July 1969. Bernard Lonergan Archive, TR 69 4B/ 52200DTE060. https://bernardlonergan.com/archive/52200dte060/.
– "Religious Commitment." In *The Pilgrim People of God: A Vision with Hope*, edited by Joseph Papin, 45–70. Villanova, PA: Villanova University Press, 1970.
– *A Second Collection*. Edited by Robert M. Doran and John D. Dadosky. Vol. 13 of *Collected Works of Bernard Lonergan*. Toronto: University of Toronto Press, 2016.
– *A Third Collection*. Edited by Robert M. Doran and John D. Dadosky. Vol. 16 of *Collected Works of Bernard Lonergan*. Toronto: University of Toronto Press, 2017.

- *Topics in Education: The Cincinnati Lectures of 1959 on the Philosophy of Education.* Edited by Robert M. Doran and Frederick E. Crowe. Revised and augmented by James Quinn and John Quinn. Vol. 10 of *Collected Works of Bernard Lonergan.* Toronto: University of Toronto Press, 1993.
- *The Triune God: Systematics.* Edited by Robert M. Doran and H. Daniel Monsour. Translated by Michael G. Shields. Vol. 12 of *Collected Works of Bernard Lonergan.* Toronto: University of Toronto Press, 2007.
- *Understanding and Being: The Halifax Lectures on Insight.* Edited by Elizabeth A. Morelli and Mark D. Morelli. Revised and augmented by Frederick E. Crowe with the collaboration of Elizabeth A. Morelli, Mark D. Morelli, Robert M. Doran, and Thomas V. Dally. Vol. 5 of *Collected Works of Bernard Lonergan.* Toronto: University of Toronto Press, 1990.
- *Verbum: Word and Idea in Aquinas.* Edited by Frederick E. Crowe and Robert M. Doran. Vol. 2 of *Collected Works of Bernard Lonergan.* Toronto: University of Toronto Press, 1997.

Loyola, Ignatius of. *The Spiritual Exercises of St. Ignatius.* Translated by George Ganss, SJ. St. Louis, MO: Institute of Jesuit Sources, 1992.

Merton, Thomas. *Contemplation in a World of Action.* Garden City, NY: Doubleday, 1965.

Nasr, Seyyed Hossein. Foreword to *Divine Love: Islamic Literature and the Path to God,* by William Chittick, ii–xx. New Haven, CT: Yale University Press, 2013

Newman, John Henry. *An Essay in Aid of a Grammar of Assent.* London: Burns and Oates, 1870.

Ogbonnaya, Joseph. *Lonergan, Social Transformation, and Sustainable Human Development.* Eugene, OR: Pickwick, 2013.

O'Hara, J. Martin, ed. *Curiosity at the Center of One's Life: Statements and Questions of Eric O'Connor.* Montreal: Thomas More Institute, 1987.

Orji, Cyril. "Are There Stages of Meaning in African Theology?" *Toronto Journal of Theology* 32, no. 1 (Spring 2016): 71–93. https://doi.org/10.3138/tjt.3685.

Panikkar, Raimon. *The Intrareligious Dialogue.* New York: Paulist Press, 1999.

Peck, M. Scott. *The Road Less Traveled: A New Psychology of Love, Traditional Values, and Spiritual Growth.* 25th anniversary edition. New York: Touchstone, 2003.

Polanyi, Michael. *Personal Knowledge.* London: Routledge and Kegan Paul, 1962.

Price, George. *The Narrow Pass: A Study of Kierkegaard's Concept of Man.* London: Hutchinson, 1963.

Raab, Joseph Q. "Encountering Others: Interpreting the Faith Development of Thomas Merton in Light of Fowler's 'Stages of Development.'" *Religious Education* 94, no. 2 (Spring 1992): 140–54. https://doi.org/10.1080/0034408990940202.

Rahner, Karl. *Foundations of Christian Faith.* Translated by W. Dych. New York: Crossroad, 1987.

- "Towards a Fundamental Interpretation of Vatican II." *Theological Studies* 40, no. 4 (1979): 716–27. https://doi.org/10.1177/004056397904000404.
Sala, Giovanni. *Lonergan and Kant: Five Essays on Human Knowledge*. Toronto: University of Toronto Press, 1994.
Saracino, Michele. *On Being Human: A Conversation with Lonergan and Levinas*. Marquette Studies in Theology 35. Milwaukee, WI: Marquette University Press, 2003.
Scheler, Max. *Ressentiment*. Edited by Lewis A. Coser. Translated by William W. Holdheim. New York: Free Press of Glencoe, 1961.
Simmel, Georg. "Die Wendung zur Idee." In *Lebensanschauung: Vier metaphsysiche Kaptitel*, 29–98. Munich: Duncker and Humblot, 1918.
Snell, Bruno. *The Discovery of the Mind: The Greek Origins of European Thought*. Translated by Thomas G. Rosenmeyer. New York: Harper Torchbook, 1960.
Tambiah, Stanley J. *Magic, Science, Religion, and the Scope of Rationality*. Cambridge: Cambridge University Press, 1990.
Tracy, David. *The Achievement of Bernard Lonergan*. New York: Herder and Herder, 1970.
Vertin, Michael. "Judgments of Value, for the Later Lonergan." *Method: Journal of Lonergan Studies* 13, no. 2 (Fall 1995): 221–48. https://doi.org/10.5840/method19951327.
von Balthasar, Hans Urs. "Revelation and the Beautiful." In *The Word Made Flesh*, vol. 1 of *Theological Explorations*, 95–126. San Francisco: Ignatius Press, 1989.
Whelan, Gerard. *A Discerning Church: Pope Francis, Lonergan, and a Theological Method for the Future*. Mahwah, NJ: Paulist Press, 2019.
Whitson, Robley Edward. *The Coming Convergence of World Religions*. New York: Newman, 1971.

Index

Alexander, Christopher, 76
Arasteh, Reza, 120
Aristotle, 11, 23, 105
art, 49, 51, 55, 76–7, 79, 80, 82, 89, 138n6, 138n13, 139n20
Athanasius, 5
authenticity, 5, 21, 57–8, 71, 82, 101, 102, 117, 135n5

Balthasar, Hans Urs von, 35, 95, 104, 107, 117
beauty: the beautiful, xi, 31–5, 48–9, 57, 76, 99, 104, 106, 109, 138n9, 143–4nn15–16; as transcendental, 6, 32–4
being in love, 29, 53, 91–3, 97–9, 103–9, 112–13, 115–19, 125, 141n10; acts of loving, 3; first principle, 94; with God 97, 102–4, 106, 116, 119; unrestricted, 92, 98–9, 106–7, 109, 118–19, 125. *See also* grace: sanctifying
belief(s): context of, 65; faith and, 101, 114, 116; immanently generated knowledge, 64–5, 69; in *Insight*, 64–6, 68–9; in *Method*, 68
bias: dramatic, 6, 54, 72, 125, 144n1; general, 72, 90, 125; group, 72; individual (egoistic), 72

Binswanger, Ludwig, 28
Buddhism, 108, 139n27, 141n11, 143n14
Butterfield, Herbert, 17
Byrne, Patrick, 138–9nn15–17, 139n20, 140n45

Camus, Albert, 101–2, 143n7
Cano, Melchior, 18
Catholic theology, 3, 19
Chittick, William, 108
church, xiii, 3–4, 15–17, 20, 123–4, 128, 130, 134n15
classicist notion of culture, 9, 17, 18, 19–20, 21–22, 139n21, 141n11
cognitional theory, 26, 38, 39, 42, 87, 129
common sense, 5, 11, 14, 20, 36, 46, 78, 83–6, 88–99, 111, 114–18, 123
communications, as inculturation, 10, 111, 126
community of feeling, 74
conscience, 44, 47, 55–6, 59, 61, 95
consciousness: consolation/desolation as indicating correct judgment, 59, 61, 140n34; differentiation(s) of, 5, 11, 21, 31, 33–4, 46–7, 83, 92, 141–2n17; empirical, 136n10; as experience, 29, 76, 81, 104; fifth level, 29, 52, 99, 118–19, 141n10;

consciousness (*continued*)
  intentional, 5, 8, 11, 22, 26, 29–30, 32, 35–6, 38–9, 42, 52, 79, 89, 91, 98, 101–2, 112, 115, 117–18, 135n4; interiorly differentiated, 86; levels of, xii, 48, 52, 55, 79, 83, 89, 127–8, 136n10; undifferentiated, 88–90
consolation/desolation, indicating correct judgment, 59, 61, 140n34
context: of belief, 65; of community, 13, 78, 123, 127; of cooperation, 45; of decisions, 58–9; cultural, 14, 108; Ignatian, 60; Jesuit, 9; new, xi, 17, 100, 116; philosophical, 20, 86–7; pluralistic, 3–6; relevance for understanding outer word, 111; Western, 141
contextual theology, 10, 17, 18–19
conversion: intellectual, 85, 94, 125; moral, 48, 125; psychological (psychic), 55, 77, 124, 139n28, 144n1. *See also* being in love
Crowe, Frederick, 3, 60, 62–3, 89, 106, 142n26, 143n14, 144n17
culture: classical, 23–24; classicist, 9, 17–22, 135n24, 139n21, 141n11; empirical notion, 7, 17–21, 116; function of, 50

Dadosky, John, 134n16
Danto, Arthur, 138n13
data: of consciousness, 28, 30, 36–7, 80, 86, 118; and functional specialization, 3, 7, 100, 122, 133n1 (introduction); research, 11, 22, 24, 122
Dawson, Christopher, 19
decision: and commitment, xii, 9, 13, 16, 26, 52–3, 59, 71, 82–3, 93, 102, 106, 112, 116, 118–19, 124–5, 141n10; and conscience, 44, 47, 55–6, 59, 61, 95; and deliberation; 29, 32, 44, 48, 55–7, 59, 61–2, 80–1, 88, 92, 101–2, 104, 115, 138n15; and dialectic, 3, 5–6, 11, 13, 22, 38, 49, 68, 98, 110, 119, 122–3, 126, 128–31, 139n19; and foundations, xi, 3, 5–6, 11, 22, 41, 122, 124–6, 128–31, 144n3; and will, 61, 62, 63
decline, 17, 20, 45, 58, 71–3, 83. *See also* progress
de Finance, Joseph, 58
demythologization, 16, 17, 68
Descartes, René, 86, 91
development: and breakdowns, 51; and differentiations, 5, 21, 33, 46–7, 83, 89–90, 92, 94; and Piaget, 45–6, 138n6
dialectic and conversion, 123–6, 131
Die Wendung zur Idee, 132
differentiation(s) of consciousness, 11, 21; and knowledge, 5; and patterns of experience, 33; and religion, 92; and stages of meaning, 31, 46–7, 83; and theology, 5; types of, 34, 141–2n17
discernment, as methodological principle, 17
doctrine(s): as functional specialty, 122, 124–6, 130–1; types of, 16, 86–7, 111, 134n6, 144n17
dogma(s), 17, 21, 128
Doran, Robert, xii, 6, 10, 11, 14–16, 44–5, 52, 59–63, 77–8, 125, 133n1 (introduction), 139nn28–9, 140n39, 141n15, 142n20
Doyle, Dennis, xi, 142n20
dreams, 27
Dyer, Mary, 19

education, 4, 13–14, 18, 46, 68, 70, 89, 131, 138n6
egoism, individual and group, 29
Eliade, Mircea, 77
emergent probability, 12–13

emotional identification, and intersubjectivity, 74–5
empiricism, 86
exigence(s), 60, 84–6, 88, 91–2, 94–9, 117–18
experience, as source for theology, 19
experiencing-understanding-judging-deciding, xi, 5, 25, 27, 115. *See also* knowing: as experiencing, understanding, judging
expression: and art, 49, 51, 55, 76–7, 79–80, 82, 84, 89, 138n10, 138n13, 139n20; of religious experience, 109–10, 113–14

faith, as knowledge born of religious love, 112
feeling(s): of conscience, 44, 47, 55–6, 59, 61, 95; respond to objects in two ways, 48; role in value apprehension, 47, 57, 112, 140n39, 140n44; transcendental, 53
fellow-feeling, 76
foundations, as functional specialty, 108, 124–6
fourth level, 6, 29–30, 33, 41, 44, 55–6, 112, 114–15, 118–19, 141n7, 141n10. *See also* decision
fourth stage of meaning, 83, 88–95, 97, 99–100, 103, 116–17, 119–20, 142n21
Fowler, James, 93, 110, 119
Fox, George, 19
freedom, 8, 14, 16, 24, 29, 38, 44, 58–9, 76, 135n4, 143n7
Frye, Northrop, 77
functional specialties: and levels of consciousness, xii, 48, 52, 55, 79, 83, 89, 127, 128, 136n10

Galatians: *5:13*, 115; *5:22–3*, 108, 109
Galileo, 16, 24, 96

Gefühl, 19
Girard, René, 49, 54, 72, 99, 109–11
God: gift of love, 95, 108, 113, 114, 116–17 (*see also* being in love: with God; religious experience; transcendence: and God); question of, 101–2
good: always concrete, 45; in *Insight*, 44–5, 60–1, 68–9, 72, 100, 137n1; of order; 50, 52, 70–1; particular, 50, 52, 70–1. *See also* human good; value(s)
grace: and being in love with God, 29, 53, 91–9, 97, 99, 102–9, 112–13, 115–16, 118–19; and religious conversion, 93, 123–5; sanctifying, 104, 105, 115

Harnack, Adolf von, 145n4
Harris, Marvin, 18
heart, 108, 111, 112, 113, 131
Hegel, G.W.F., 11, 13, 38, 111
Heidegger, Martin, 26, 42
Heiler, Friedrich, 106–7, 110, 143–4n15, 144n16
heuristic structures/function, 39, 41–2, 129
history, different senses of, 20
human good: components in, 45; structure of , 56, 70–1
Hume, David, 38, 86

idealism, 11, 58
ideology, 72, 75, 112
immediacy, mediated return to, 81
inculturation, 126. *See also* communications, as inculturation; mediation
insight(s): deliberative, 60, 63–4; direct, 140n39; evaluative, 64; reflective, 25, 63–4, 79, 140n39. *See also* understanding

intellect, 28, 67–8, 115, 136n10, 140n44
intelligibility: anticipation of, 30; classical and statistical, 23–4; demand for, 91, 95; and fourth stage of meaning, 97; as potential, 63, 79, 80; as transcendental, 32, 34–5, 49, 55, 95, 138n12; of universe, 101
intending, different levels, 29–32, 95
intentionality, analysis of, 27, 29–32, 35–6, 39, 55, 102–3
interiority, and turn to the subject, 20, 86–8, 91, 95
interiorly differentiated consciousness, 86
internal communication, 77
interpretation, as functional specialty, 3, 5–6, 11, 16, 22, 75, 105, 116, 122–3, 126–9
intersubjectivity, 48–50, 74–5, 139n19
introspection, 27–8
isomorphism, 39

Jesuits in Canada, 9
Johnson, Robert A., 37
judgment: and absolute, 19; common-sense, 88; criterion of, 56, 66
judgments: and truth, 57, 138n10; of value (*see* value(s): judgments of)
Jung, Carl, 37, 77

Kant, Immanuel, 56, 86, 136–7n15
Kierkegaard, Søren, 51, 100–1, 103–4, 112
kleshas, 139n27
knowing: as experiencing, understanding, judging, 5, 31–2, 35–6, 39–40, 52, 87, 104, 112, 114, 124, 129; fragmentation of knowledge, 3–4, 20–1, 87, 121, 128

Langer, Susanne, 60, 76
language, ordinary, 137n19
laws: classical, 23–4; statistical, 23–4
learning, as self-correcting process, 84
levels of consciousness, and functional specialties, xii, 48, 52, 55, 79, 83, 89, 127–8, 136n10. *See also* consciousness; fourth level
Lévy-Bruhl, Lucien, 89, 141–2n17
liberty: and growth, 58; horizontal, 58; vertical, 58–9
Locke, John, 18
logic, 77–8, 81
Lonergan, Bernard: *CWL 3*, 12, 14, 23, 46, 49, 54, 60, 65–8, 87; *CWL 5*, 46; *CWL 6*, 11–13, 14–15; *CWL 7*, 28, 136n10; *CWL 10*, 51–2, 85; *CWL 13*, 5, 17, 19, 27, 44, 62; *CWL 14* (*Method in Theology*), 27, 33, 70, 114, 132; *CWL 16*, 96, 98, 112–13, 135n4; *CWL 17*, 108, 119; *CWL 18*, 46; *CWL 24*, 14; *CWL 25*, 8; "Mediation of Christ in Prayer," 12, 14; "Religious Commitment," 112, 119; "Theology in Its New Context," xi, 17
love: in relation to knowledge, 103, 106–8; romantic, 97, 144n24. *See also* being in love
Loyola, Ignatius of, xi, 4, 29, 59, 61–2, 93, 105

Massignon, Louis, 110, 144n20
McEnroy, Carmel, xi, 133n1 (preface)
McGrath, Jack, xii
meaning: acts of, 79–81; carriers of, 80; communicative, 82; constitutive, 82; effective, 80; elemental, 76, 79, 137n19; first stage of, 84, 98, 105, 114; fourth

stage of, 83, 88, 90–5, 97, 99, 100, 103, 116–17, 119–20, 142n21; functions of, 81; realms of, 11, 21, 83, 86, 91, 114; stages of, 20, 74, 83–4, 91–2, 94, 96–7, 105, 111; stages of outside Western context, 141n11
mediation: and immediacy, 81, 88, 111, 125; mutual self-mediation, 15; as two-way street, 14–15, 21; world mediated by meaning, 81, 125
Merton, Thomas, 110, 117, 119–20, 141n11
metaphysics, 4, 39, 42, 86–7
method: generalized empirical, 5, 14, 21, 24, 40, 88–9, 97–8, 137n16; three ways of conceiving, 60; transcendental, 24–5, 35–6, 40–3, 88, 96–7, 137n16
mind, 18, 24, 30, 35, 38, 40, 41, 42, 65, 69, 77, 79, 85, 90, 113; corrupt, 73; philosophy of, 87
model, 22, 126
modernity, and historical mindedness, 113
Monsour, H. Daniel, 133n3 (preface)
mystery, 4, 53, 105, 111
mysticism, 46, 82, 94, 95, 113, 142n17
myth/mythic consciousness, 27, 84, 96, 109, 114, 124

Newman, John Henry, 47
Nietzsche, Friedrich, 54
nihil amatum nisi praecognitum, 115
non-intentional states and trends, 47

objectification, 30, 76, 114, 117, 124
objectivity, 87
object(s): and beauty, 32–5, 138n10; and beliefs, 68–9; conscious operations as, 28, 36, 80, 98; and description, 84; and feelings, 47–9, 57, 74–5, 77; and functional specialties, 129, 138n10; intended, 39; of inquiry, 42, 91; and level of understanding, 39; no apprehended, 92, 108, 116; proportionate to, 26–7, 29; related to subject or community, 97–8; and symbols, 77; of theology, 22, 40; of thought, 80; and utilitarianism, 76
Ogbonnaya, Joseph, 52
operations: basic pattern of, 24, 25, 31; and conversion, 124; and skills, 45–6, 70–1. *See also* pattern(s)
order of teaching and order of discovery, 128
orientation, 35, 40, 52, 70–1, 82, 89, 94, 103, 119, 131, 142n17
Origen, 5, 137n21
Orji, Cyril, xii, 141n11

Panikkar, Raimondo, 110
pattern(s): basic pattern of operations, 24; experiential pattern, 76; formally dynamic, of operations, 32; link between patterns and differentiations (Piaget), 46; materially dynamic, of operations, 31
Paul, St., 104–6, 108
Peck, M. Scott, 125
phase(s) of theology, mediating and mediated, 5, 11, 128, 132
phenomenology, 75. *See also* smile: and elemental meaning
philosophy, 22, 38, 42, 91, 138n6; Aristotle's, 105; of beauty, 49; of consciousness, 38; of culture, 139n21; of education, 46; of history, 20, 135n24; of knowledge, 7–8; Lonergan's, 8, 14, 25, 35, 42, 49, 56, 59–60, 136–7n15; mistaken, 5;

philosophy (*continued*)
  Plato's, 118; and problem of evil, 42; and questions, 41–2; and stages of meaning, 85–90, 91; and theology 4, 42, 96; and Wittgenstein, 137n19
Piaget, Jean, 45, 46, 138n6
pluralism, 3–6, 20, 21, 73, 103
Polanyi, Michael, 86
polytheism, 105
Pope Francis, 117
presence, 21, 27, 59, 108
principle(s), and foundations, 122, 124, 126, 128. *See also* foundations, as functional specialty
priora quod se/priora quod nos, 115
progress, 20, 45, 55, 71, 73, 78, 89, 91. *See also* decline
psychological present, 27

questioning, 37, 87, 91, 101–2, 104
question(s): and self-transcendence, 102; for deliberation, 32, 44, 56, 61; for intelligence, 101, 102; limiting question's bound in fields of inquiry, 41–2; for reflection, 32; relevant question and judgment, 37, 67, 87; three basic questions, 42

Rahner, Karl, xi, 4–5
real, the, 24, 28, 30, 35, 39, 77, 80–1, 107, 124
reality and knowing, 38, 57–8, 80
reason, 19, 47, 89, 112, 115, 127
redemption, 20, 58, 73, 110
reflection, xi, 127
Regis College: lectures, 34–5, 114, 125, 144n25; and Lonergan, 8
relations, personal, and human good, 70
religion: as differentiated realm, 94, 118; genuine, 3, 83, 91, 96, 100–1, 103, 106, 109, 110, 113, 117–18, 143n14; transcultural basis of, 91
religious experience, 19, 74, 101, 104, 105, 106, 111, 114, 115, 118
research, as functional specialty, 6, 11, 22, 122–7
responsibility, 35, 38, 49, 82, 93, 115, 117
ressentiment, 54
revision, 36, 39, 65

Sala, Giovanni, 136–7n15
Scheler, Max, 47, 50, 54, 60, 74
Schleiermacher, Friedrich, 19
science, 5, 10, 16–18, 20, 22–5, 28, 33–4, 38, 41, 83–6, 96, 118, 121
Second Vatican Council/Vatican II, xi, 3–4, 15–17, 19–20, 130
secularism, 21
self-appropriation, 41
self-transcendence. *See under* transcendence
shenpa, 139n27
Simmel, George, 132
sin, and alienation, 55, 72, 78
skills, and human good, 45–6, 70–1, 122
smile, and elemental meaning, 75–6, 80
Snell, Bruno, 96
socialization, and acculturation/education, 18
social science(s), xiii, 17–18, 23, 87
specialization, field, 121–2, 129, 132. *See also* functional specialties
Spiritual Exercises, 29, 59–60, 105, 112. *See also* Loyola, Ignatius
stages of meaning. *See* meaning: stages of
Starkloff, Carl, xii
subject, psychologic, 26
subjectivity, 34–5, 87

symbols: and aesthetic, 78; as carrier of meaning, 77–8, 125
systematics, as functional specialty, 3, 5–6, 9–11, 22, 41, 74, 122–31, 133n1 (introduction)
systematic theology, 8, 10, 78, 87, 95

Tambiah, Stanley J., 141–2n17
technical terms, 9
Teresa of Avila, 112
terms and relations, 22
Tertullian, 5, 137n21
theologian: comparative, 131; and foundations, 124; and functional specialization, 122, 127; Lonergan on operations of, 22; mediation by, 15–16; and transcendental method, 40–3; and interiority, 95. *See also* theology
theology, 3–11, 13–22, 32–4, 39–40, 42–3, 117, 124–6, 128–9; Catholic, 3, 19; contextual, 10, 17, 18–19; and differentiation of consciousness, 5; "done on one's knees," 117; experience as source, 19; and interiority, 114–15; and Lonergan, 56, 87, 100, 121–2, 135n24; systematic, 8, 10, 78, 87, 95; task of, 91
theoretically differentiated consciousness, 86, 91
theory: and common sense, 5, 86, 88, 90–1, 97–8, 111, 114; and practice, 125; as realm of meaning, 85–6
Thomas Aquinas, 7–8, 62–3, 87, 95, 100, 105
Tracy, David, 8
tradition, xi, 15–16, 19, 82, 90, 93–4, 105, 110–11, 113, 119, 130–1
transcendence: and beauty, 34; deviated, 111; differing views of, 42; and feelings, 53–4; as fourth stage of meaning, 90–9; and God, 53, 101–2; over-emphasis on, 108, 109; psychological, 125; self-transcendence, 34, 50, 51, 53, 57, 58, 71, 98, 101–2, 115, 117, 135n4 (*see also* value: personal); and religion, 52; realm of, 83, 84, 88, 111, 114, 117, 119–20
transcendental(s): and beauty, 6, 32–5, 49; categorial vs., 38; in Kantian sense, 136–7n15; method, 24–5, 35–6, 40–3, 88, 96–7, 137n16; notions, 30–2, 34, 40, 42, 55, 71; precepts, xii, 36, 41, 55, 57–8, 72–3, 137
truth, of judgments, 57, 138n10

ultimate concern, 92
unauthenticity, 82
unconditioned, the: 64–70, 81, 87–8, 91; God as, 101
unconsciousness, 27, 53, 55, 72
understanding, 5, 33, 71, 138; acts of, 79–80, 85; vs. conception, 136n8; of doctrines, 125, 127; explanatory, 115; and faith, 9, 16; and Locke, 18; mediation of, 16; of the mysteries, 10; as operation (level of), 25–30, 32, 35–7, 39, 40, 48, 52, 81, 83, 87, 91, 93, 98, 101, 102, 104, 112, 114, 118, 124, 128, 129, 136n10; oriented to, 72; of outer word, 111; and preferential scale, 52; pursuit of, 115; questions for, 32, 37; reflective act of, 66–7; scientific pursuit of, 31, 32; self-, 13, 17, 29; and systematics, 125, 127; of truth, 57; of world process, 85
unrestricted being in love, 92, 98–9, 106–7, 109, 118–19, 125

value(s): cultural, 3, 50–2, 139n20; judgments of, 44–5, 56–9, 61, 63–5, 67, 69, 112, 125, 137n1,

value(s) (*continued*)
140n39, 140nn44–5; notion of, 55, 59–60; personal, 51–2, 118, 144n28; personal, as committed love, friendship, vocation, 51–2, 59, 144n28; religious, 52, 112, 118; scale of, 49, 52–4, 58, 118; social, 50–2; vital, 50–2, 138–9n16

Vertin, Michael, 63

Von Hildebrand, Dietrich, 47, 50, 60

Wendung zur Idee, 132

Wesley, Charles, 19

Whitson, Robley Edward, 93, 142n22

will and conscience, 55–6, 59, 61

wisdom, 3–4, 21, 25, 27, 33, 69, 84, 113, 116, 121, 132

Wittgenstein, Ludwig, 38, 137n19

word, as expression of religious experience, 111

Milton Keynes UK
Ingram Content Group UK Ltd.
UKHW030702021124
450385UK00002B/11/J